DON'T GO BACK
TO SLEEP

A Memoir

By Lisa Barstow

Lisa Barstow

Library of Congress Control Number: 2009924790

Cover Art:

Lingua Series (Radiants) is a work by artist Grace DeGennaro
(www.gracedegennaro.com)
It is from a large series in gouache and watercolor on Okawara paper. On
a ground of transparent color the central image is rendered through a
deliberate accretion of beads of color. The seed of the form is both con-
tained and reflected in the final shape, growth through the passage of
time made visible.

Rainbow River Press

FOR MY CHILDREN

Sabrina, Elise and Adrian

and my grand children

STORIES

WITH MY GRATITUDE TO:

Tom Absher, my creative writing professor at Vermont College, who oversaw my senior project in the year 2000. Although I didn't know it at the time, the project was my first draft. Tom helped me to believe that my voice had a place in the world.

Joan Hunter, my writing coach, mentor, and friend. Joan encouraged me to persevere when I wanted to "be done with it." Her writing retreat center, Fifth House Lodge in Maine, provided me with a quiet place to write and the space to move forward. Her coaching lent invaluable insight on the book's earlier structure and form.

Barbara Delage, whose friendship and professional expertise have helped make this book a reality. She has seen this through from beginning to end and I could not have done it without her.

Celia Jeffries, my editor, who pointed out that the draft I sent her, was, in fact, a draft, and not the final copy. She encouraged me to write more of my story, and then added her expert editing skills and positive feedback.

Kristina Morgan, who proof read line by line, and taught me some grammar "rules."

Anne Landgraf and Susan Miller at Brooklyn Bookworks and Rebecca Humrich at Sheridan Books. They have taken my stories and created a beautiful book.

Cynthia Barstow, my sister-in-law, who, several years ago, gave me a Christmas gift of the courage to move forward.

Grace DeGennaro, my friend, and the artist whose work has 'graced' the cover.

Patricia Lee Lewis and Ani Tuzman whose groups I attended gave me the writing practice I needed to begin to call myself "a writer."

My writing group in Maine: Heather Davis, Polly Nodden, Jan Hryniewicz, Eve McPheeters, Deirdre Drennen, and Beth Baskin. They are all wonderful, encouraging women who kept asking how my book was going, read earlier drafts, and cheered me on.

The old "group" in Maine (you know who you are). This book wouldn't have been as much fun to write without the summer memories we all share.

Meredith Jordan and Deborah Pfeffer, my beautiful 'writer' friends, and all the **'Dreamers.**

Dear, dear "sister" friends: Nan Carey, Peg Holcomb, Sally Singingtree, and Glenny Dunbar. Your love and wise counsel mean more to me than I can truly express in words.

My loving Stonecliff family. Especially Aunt Anne, who holds the honored position of elder of our clan.

My heart fills to bursting when I feel the love and encouragement of my entire family, especially my three children, **Sabrina, Elise, and Adrian.** You are an unending source of inspiration to me.

My gratitude, and so much more, to **my husband Bill,** who shows me myself over and over again. His patience and abiding love have helped me to learn more about loving myself, and that has empowered me to write my story.

~

The breeze at dawn has secrets to tell you;
don't go back to sleep.
You must ask for what you really want;
don't go back to sleep.
People are going back and forth across the doorsill
where the two worlds touch.
The door is round and open.
Don't go back to sleep.

—*Rumi*

FOREWORD

WHEN I NAMED MY MEMOIR after Rumi's poem I had no idea just how appropriate and prophetic it would be. Writing my story has continually necessitated a journey "back and forth across the doorsill, where the two worlds touch." I have had to coax the memories that lay deep inside my cells out into the light. Many of them didn't exist until I began the process of writing—thus began a journey between the worlds of the conscious and unconscious. Once more of my story was revealed I dove into deeper layers and found more truth. I began to understand that I have tried to stay awake and not go back to sleep in this lifetime, to live as consciously as my courage would allow.

Writing this book has given me an opportunity to step back and be my own witness, to see the multiple designs that have been woven by the threads that connect my life's experience and to view the entire tapestry that has become the picture of my life. Staying awake enables conscious participation in the creation of the design and will bring me more awareness when I make mistakes. With more clarity I can choose to alter and transform the design and weave in new, more durable threads.

I began this book eight years ago as a senior project for my creative writing class in college. Since then, I have written many drafts, and each time I deluded myself into thinking I was done. A few years ago I needed distance from my memoir, and I wrapped the manuscript up in a bright blue silk scarf and put it away for a while. When I brought it out again I realized that I no longer liked, or even agreed with, much of what I had written. So I deleted, added, edited, and deleted some more. Like a seed that is planted, germinates, roots, and sprouts, the stories written have needed nurturing and time to grow me into more consciousness. Although it will never feel completed, because there is so much more conscious living to be done, I need to let it go now. I am ready to release it, like the prayers in Tibetan prayer flags, story by story, out into the world. I pray that the story of my life thus far will find its place on currents of wind to become a part of the design of the larger whole.

Last year I found a photograph of my great-grandmother as a young woman. I had never seen her before. Staring at her face, I tried to find some familial likeness, but mostly, I wondered who she was and what she believed in. I knew then that I was writing this memoir for my grandchildren and for the generations that will come after them. I want to leave them a legacy, the story of an ancestor whose blood is mingled with theirs. There is a saying in Hawaii that I love: "We are the descendants of our ancestors, and the ancestors of our descendants." Sharing my heart with the past and future generations of my family is an honor.

God bless them all.

MY TRUTH

EXPECTATIONS WERE A LARGE PART of my upbringing. They came with the privileged WASP territory that surrounded me for much of my life. My earliest recollection of a family expectation was to be a good girl. As I grew up I began to understand that "good" meant be polite, happy, pretty, thin, popular at school, never pouting, and trying not to talk about any feelings I had that would offend others. As they stand, these expectations have merit, and some have been wonderful guides for a positive attitude and a productive life. But in my family of origin they came with conditions that held the outer, "looking good" appearances as top priority. These were the realms of my childhood that WASPs traveled in with such ease. I realize now that although charm and graciousness count for a lot in certain circumstances, they start losing their importance when you begin to "wake up" and question what those expectations actually mean. Over time, I learned that if I wanted to find my true self I had to go through the dark night of the soul and be willing to surrender who I thought I was. I turned to God when no one else would listen or understand, and I was too young to know that my parents were trying, without much success, to navigate through their own dark times. When they were suffering too much to be present and I needed someone to listen I turned to prayer and asked God for help.

I don't ever remember a time that I didn't believe in God. He was the grandfather I never knew, the person for whom I was really being good, the all-knowing man in heaven who "expected" His children to do what He said in the Bible. During my childhood years God was the Father of all expectations, and I believed if I lived up to them I would probably get what I wanted. I developed a belief that people in my social-economic class were entitled to good fortune, so naturally, trusting that God was on our side helped create an illusion of safety, security, and the feeling of being blessed. I am amazed and somewhat ashamed to find that when I look deep down into my heart as a child I believed the privileged class was privileged because, OK, I'll say it, God loved us best. But only if we were good.

I moved between darkness and light as a child when both my parents had life-threatening cancers and my grandmother died. Then as a teenager when my parents divorced, and as a young adult when they both died. Then again, ten years later when my first husband died. During those difficult periods, I still hung tightly to the belief that if I prayed hard enough God would make everything better. My childhood faith was tested when He didn't answer my prayers, but I understand now that God did send me grace.

As a more awakened adult, I feel much comfort with Spirit by my side. I have been provided with the grace I needed to help me during dark times; when I white-knuckle through the despair, I feel the softening presence of hope mingling with God's enduring light. I have been lifted to a place where I intuitively know I am held and protected by something much larger than I. I have come to an understanding that when it is time to venture outside the confines of my provincial mind, I do so because self and Spirit are asking me not to go back to sleep. I have tried to follow my intuition, which I am sure is God in action, and stepping into new and challenging territory reminds me that God holds me in an embrace of unconditional love.

A few years ago I had a vivid dream. I was on a dock and a woman walked up to me. She had just returned home from a solo voyage around the world in her small sailboat. As I took her hand and welcomed her back, I looked into her eyes and said, "Now, I want you to teach me about courage." Writing this book is teaching me about having the courage to tell the truth, as I see it, and that the way I have interpreted it is valid and my own to claim. My courage is found in the willingness to be present for myself and to shatter the illusions of my past.

After a long and sometimes frightening journey sailing around my own personal world, I recognize myself as the woman with whom I want to spend the final part of my life. My voice will continue to speak the truth of my soul.

GRATITUDE

June 2007

As I write this I am sitting on the *lanai* in our house on the island of Kauai. Bill, my second husband, and I moved from
Maine to Hawaii six months ago. Bill has taken a position as
operations manager on a family tree farm. Our brother-in-law
began planting the trees in 1992, the year we were married.

The late afternoon light is shining on the banana trees in
my yard. Their large serrated leaves move slightly in the soft
breeze and reveal a cluster of bananas that are ripening on the
trunk. Once they are picked the tree will die and a new stalk
will begin to grow out of the old one that has been hosting the
fruit. I cannot help but be reminded that when we bear fruit
often something old in us has to die, and yet, there is always
new growth in its place.

A garden spider wove such a large web on the *lanai* the other
day that Bill and I couldn't pass by without breaking it. We
decided to give the spider room for her web and I watched her
for days, as she caught smaller bugs and wrapped them up in
tiny cocoons. Then yesterday, Bill was too busy to remember
the spider and her home, and he walked straight into it. We
watched in horror as the delicate silk strands dissolved into the
air and the spider skittered off the edge of the porch. A few

days later, I was doing the dishes and looked out the window above the sink. There, right in the center of the pane, was a garden spider and a new web. (I am convinced it was the same spider we so rudely displaced!) She had positioned herself so that it appeared she was staring right at me, as if to say "I'm back!" The natural world, like us, is extremely resilient. Lives can be ruined and souls can be restored.

I am living in a paradise that provides a bounty of beauty and nourishment that feed my soul every day. But what of the places on the earth that are dry and brittle, water and new growth absent from the landscape? What about the refugees, who flow like the earth's blood, seeking a home? What about the children who are starving? There are no fruit trees in their yard. I am just as energetically connected to them, my human sisters and brothers, as I am to these trees and spiders and to all this beauty. But how do I make sense of the disparity? Why is my life surrounded by blessings? Is there an answer to the "why" that I ask?

I believe the answer is gratitude. If I have been blessed with this reality for a while, then I must remember gratitude in the moment of every day. I feel gratitude in this moment that the people I love, including myself, are healthy. I feel gratitude that I have people to love and who love me in return. I am grateful I have a warm and loving connection to Spirit, and that I learn so much from the natural world. Most important, however, is for me to remember gratitude when things do not work out as planned. To remember there is always something more to be learned in the process of living this human existence. Gratitude can serve as a bright light when I feel confused or surrounded by darkness. I am comforted when I remember to be grateful because at the core of all this gratitude is the abiding Spirit of God.

MANHATTAN

MY STORY BEGAN SIXTY-THREE YEARS ago in New York City. The years I lived there serve as a beginning, but certainly not an end. New York has a way of defining you, no matter what borough or neighborhood you grow up in, and living on Sutton Place in Manhattan for twenty years had a strong impact on my life.

Only seven blocks long, Sutton Place is a small residential enclave that is still known as a quiet, gracious location for the wealthy to live without the sounds of traffic or commercialism. It parallels the East River, and runs south to north for six short blocks. The northern boundary is the 59th Street Bridge. The bridge takes travelers across to Queens, and when I was a young child in the late forties, the only reason residents of Sutton Place would have to go across the bridge to Queens was to either get to LaGuardia airport or attend the U.S. Open Tennis Tournament in Forest Hills. My mother loved to tell about the time she took my brother Lee and I on the Circle Line Tour around the island of Manhattan, and as the boat cruised past Sutton Place, the tour guide announced, "Ladies and gentlemen, we are now passing the elite Sutton Place. No children live here, only poodles and dachshunds." Hearing this, my five-year-old brother jumped up and yelled, "Hey Mister, I live there."

The fact that Marilyn Monroe and Aristotle Onassis were my neighbors didn't make up for the fact that friends and the green grass of Central Park were across town. When I began first grade at an all-girls private school many blocks uptown, the school bus didn't come as far as Sutton Place, so instead of riding the bus like everyone else, I was picked up by David, my grandmother's chauffeur, and brought home in a 1950 black Cadillac sedan. At six I was already embarrassed by the car and the chauffeur.

There was a steep hill I walked down with my governess or my mother when we went to the "swing park," a block away on York Avenue. Once on this hill you had left Sutton Place and had to travel one block under the shadow of the bridge. It felt menacing and unsafe. The cars overhead made loud thumping sounds as they went by, and after a rain, big drops of dirty water dripped off the steel girders above and splashed on my head and the pavement around me. I always pulled my governess' hand and walked as fast as I could to get to the bottom. Just outside the park I saw men who smelled like rotten apples lying on the benches. Their bodies were covered in old newspapers, and bottles in brown paper bags were nestled close to their heads.

"Are they sick? Why do they smell? Why are they sleeping during the day?"

"Bums," my governess answered me, and she would hurry us by and into the park.

My building was #30, and the front door opened into the elegant first-floor lobby where there were potted palms planted in front of a large mirror, and a black and white square tiled marble floor. The heavy front door was painted black with a big brass handle, and John, the doorman, stood at attention beside it. Out on Sutton Place an awning stretched from the door to the curb so that when cabs or limousines let people out or picked people up they wouldn't get wet if it was raining.

One time when we were five, my best friend Stevee who lived in my building invited me over to play. Her bedroom window faced Sutton Place, and while we were having a tea party with the miniature tea set her mother had brought her back from France, I decided that we should test the strength of this fine china and throw it out her eighth-story window. Stevee, who would always do what I said, agreed, and soon cups and saucers, a tiny creamer, and a teapot were flying through the air, bouncing off the awning, and smashing in bits and pieces onto Sutton Place. John, ducking the debris, shook his fist and yelled for us to stop.

"Oh dear," Stevee whimpered, far more worried than I. "We had better hide." I obeyed—it was her window and her tea set after all—and we ran into the living room to hide behind the couch. Minutes later the doorbell rang. "It's the police," I whispered to my terrified friend. "We're going to jail."

I had other friends in my building, and all of them, except Stevee, were adults who worked there: Mr. Anderson, the Norwegian superintendant, who had arrived at Stevee's apartment to scold us (instead of the imagined police) and Miss Anthony, the building's bookkeeper, who had an office down a hallway off the lobby. She smelled like gardenias. I could smell the strong perfume from the lobby, so I always knew if she was in her office and I could go visit. I loved her tropical scent, even though Mummy said it was cheap perfume. Miss Anthony's hair was dyed as black as charcoal, and she had a big mole on her chin that she penciled in black to match her hair. Her full lips and sharp, long fingernails were painted a bright crimson. Miss Anthony lived in Brooklyn so she had to travel far to get to her job. The only thing I knew about Brooklyn was that Coney Island

and the Cyclone, the world's largest roller coaster, were there. My other friends in the building were John, the kind, white-haired doorman, and Grover, who drove the front elevator.

Sometimes when my parents were out or having cocktails in the living room I'd go out into the front foyer and ring the elevator bell. A few minutes later the elevator door would open and Grover would appear.

"Can I ride with you and drive the elevator?" I'd ask him.

"Sure, for a little while," Grover grinned. He had three teeth.

The cab had a handle that was mounted on a wheel and when you moved it to the right or left it guided the elevator up and down.

"Oooh Grover," I complained, trying to do it just like him, "it is so hard to get it level with the floor." After several tries I was finally able to pull the door open and greet the people who had been waiting patiently.

"Good evening," I announced with my most polite voice and smile, "going down?"

I loved to watch my neighbors as they stepped gracefully into the elevator, the women in their fur coats and mink stoles and the men in black Chesterfield overcoats with velvet collars, white cashmere scarves draped casually around their necks. The elevator was filled with the scent of French perfume and the dazzle of gorgeous jewelry.

"May I call you a cab?" I eventually asked after I closed the door, turned the handle all the way to the left, and started going down a little too fast.

If they nodded "yes," there was a bell I'd push that rang in the lobby, signaling John to whistle for a taxi. John had a beautiful chrome whistle he blew so loudly that taxicabs many blocks away could hear it and arrive at the curb in front of the building in minutes. The sound of whistles being blown by doormen all over Sutton Place was one of things I liked best about my neighborhood.

John and Grover looked like generals in full dress. They wore deep green double-breasted wool uniforms with brass buttons. The jackets had gold epaulets with fringe on the shoulders. In the summer they changed into plain brown uniforms that weren't hot, scratchy wool. Embossed in gold across their hearts on both uniforms was *30 Sutton Place.* They wore hats with sturdy plastic visors, which they tipped cordially to anyone who came into or left the building. They had known my mother since she had moved there at the age of fourteen. Grover brought Mummy down in the elevator dressed as a bride, and a few years later John helped her out of a cab when she brought me home from the hospital.

My grandparents, Nanny and Papa, lived in my building in an elegant, two-story apartment just a few floors above my smaller, plainer one. We also lived together on the same property in Maine in the summers.

On the first floor of their duplex a large foyer connected the mahogany-paneled library with the living room and dining room that had windows looking out on the East River. I loved the river. My grandparents had the best view, but I could see a little slice of it from my bedroom window. It is not a lazy, meandering river, like the kind that flows through marshlands in Maine, but a strong river that looks like it has a sense of purpose. Nevertheless, I always felt peaceful gazing out at it. I loved to watch it transport huge barges pulled by tugboats, tour boats, and graceful sailboats up and down and around Manhattan, an island full of concrete and steel. Unlike the rivers in Maine, its banks were not made of soft damp earth. That had been covered over by asphalt years before.

Living with privilege will often gloss over what doesn't want to be seen. I was not as protected as my friends who had

moved to the suburbs, however, and once out of the confines of
Sutton Place the diversity of the city was difficult not to
notice.

Because there were no stores on Sutton Place, Mummy and
I went shopping on First Avenue or walked the several blocks
to Bloomingdales, then a houseware department store, to buy
toilet paper, brooms and mops. My favorite store in the neighborhood was Louie's, named for the friendly Italian man who
sold fruits, vegetables and assorted meats. I loved Louie and I
knew he liked me. He stood near the door to his shop greeting
his customers, and when he saw Mummy and me his face broke
into a huge grin.

"Hello, young lady, how are you today?" Louie's kind brown
eyes twinkled as he smiled at me. "You want a nice slice of
bologna?"

"Oh yes, thank you, Louie," I said, noticing his apron was
stained with peach juice and beef blood. I went inside and
stood next to the meat case looking at the lamb chops with
their frilly paper hats covering the bone. Louie handed me a
slice of bologna cut fresh from the roll that lay in the meat case
next to the salami, liverwurst, and paper-thin slices of veal. I
folded the slice in half, then again, and before I took a bite I
was careful to peel off the circle of skin that looked and felt like
a rubber band. The bologna tasted so good that I wanted to ask
for another slice, but I knew that wouldn't be polite.

Inside the busy shop an old woman who looked like a witch
sat in a glass cage. When the phone rang she answered and took
down delivery orders. Her stringy grey hair was pulled back
into a bun and every time I saw her she was wearing a black
dress and a black shawl drawn around her stooped shoulders.
Her face was full of wrinkles, like my basset hound Timmy, and
she never smiled. I was scared of her until Louie told me proudly
one day that she was his mother.

"Mummy," I asked, "why does Louie's mother look so different than your mother, Nanny?"

"Well sweetie, I imagine Louie's mother has had a hard life." She paused for a moment, then added, "She is an immigrant. She left everything she knew in the "old country" and came to America to get a new start." I didn't ask her why she decided to do that, but I suppose I understood better why she might look unhappy.

I saw many people who looked and acted very differently from me or my family. Across from Louie's, there was a family of little people who always sat together on their front stoop and an obese family around the corner who Mummy said must have glandular problems, or else why would they be so fat?

On our way to Maine every June, with my nose pressed up against the window of our two-toned red and white Plymouth wagon, I watched the kids playing in the streams of water from opened fire hydrants in Harlem. I had fleeting moments of feeling confusion and guilt, and "woke up" enough to wonder why I had a home in Maine and these kids did not. But just like the homeless "bums" on the bench outside the playground, we were always hurrying by. I was curious, but there was never time to form the questions. Even if there had been, I doubt the answers would have been compelling enough to keep me from "going back to sleep." From a child's point of view, these diverse scenes were a window into the imagination, and during my childhood, for whatever I didn't understand I made up a story that helped satisfy my curiosity.

From my bedroom I loved to watch an old lady who lived in the brownstone directly across the street from my fourth-floor window. She was always perched on her window seat like one of the pigeons that roosted on the sills, watching the street below. I noticed that she never got dressed, wearing the same house coat every day. When her legs were stretched out in front of her I could see that she had thick tan stockings rolled down, forming fat lumps around her ankles. I wondered and worried about her. I doubted she had a family or friends, not even a cat for company. *Poor old lady*, I thought as I watched her, *I'll be your friend.* What did her world look like inside the apartment? I imagined that her bedroom had an iron bed with a lumpy mattress, like the ones my grandmother's maids slept on in Maine. Was the apartment full of dust? Did it smell like burned food? Every day when I got home from school, I looked to see if she was sitting by her window. When she was there I'd stick my head out my window and stare, hoping that she'd look over and see me so I could wave at her, maybe even strike up a conversation from across the street. Then she would invite me over for tea. I would take some cookies I'd baked and she wouldn't be so alone. But she never once looked up to meet my gaze.

Beginning in early spring, when it was warm enough to open the windows, a musician came and played his violin in the courtyard of our building, directly beneath my brother's bedroom window. When Lee and I heard the music we opened the window wide, and then rushed to our piggy banks to get nickels and dimes (never pennies, Mummy said) to throw out the window, aiming for his brown cap upside down on the pavement. Soon change was flying out of the many windows facing the courtyard. Every now and then when a coin dropped beside him the fiddler stopped playing and took a small bow.

The courtyard was a bare cement square formed where the two sides of the building came together. It had a large drain in the center. One day while Lee was lying on his bed reading a comic book, a maid who lived with a family five floors above us in apartment 9A jumped out of her tiny maid's room window. Her body flew past my brother's window, landing hard in the courtyard below. Mummy and I were in the kitchen getting lunch when we heard a terrible *thunk* as the poor woman's body hit the pavement. Lee was still reading *Superman* when my mother ran into his room worried that he had seen the woman fall. When I dared to look down, my friend Mr. Anderson, the superintendent, was standing beside her, his hat in his hand. The body was covered with a brown wool blanket, and before I looked away I noticed a small stream of her bright red blood running into the drain. I was horrified. I had never seen that much blood. I couldn't stop staring at the still form under the blanket and the blood leaking out from beneath it.

"Move away from the window, Lisa," Mummy said quietly. "This is a terrible thing that has happened."

We had no idea who she was or why she was so unhappy that she had to kill herself. I thought maybe she lived far away from her family, like so many maids back then, or that her boyfriend had told her he didn't love her anymore. As I sobbed in my mother's arms, I thought about our governess, Mary McManus, who lived without her family and whose maid's room window wasn't far below the window the dead woman jumped from.

That fall my father went duck hunting on Long Island and brought six dead ducks home. Before taking them to his club to be plucked and made ready for cooking, he hung them by their necks out the kitchen window and their blood dripped into the drain in the center of the courtyard; and I imagined that the duck's blood was flowing under the pavement and mixing with the blood of the maid from apartment 9A.

During my childhood, the only times I traveled past the defined boundaries of the upper East Side and went to the West Side of the city were for horseback riding and ice skating lessons, and of course the occasional theater matinee. I didn't know anyone who lived on the other side of the Park, and when I was young I had the impression that I wouldn't want to know anyone who did. The West Side was unfamiliar and therefore somewhat frightening, and I preferred to stay where I belonged. But as I grew older I became intrigued by it. I began to assume that in order to live there, you had to be an intellectual or incredibly creative. I imagined that people who lived on the West Side read a lot and sat around their family dinner table having interesting discussions about the state of the world and the new exhibit at the Met. These were people who used their maids' rooms as studios to paint or sculpt, or to write famous novels like *Marjorie Morningstar*.

I doubted that anyone I went to dancing school with on Park Avenue came from west of Central Park, and I imagined that if the kids learned to dance it was usually with their old grandfather, who was a retired professor from Columbia and wore wire-rimmed spectacles and a rumpled sweater vest. Instead of foxtrots, their grandpas taught them polkas, and they danced together at large family gatherings to enthusiastic boisterous accordion music. I was quite sure that Cole Porter and Gershwin songs were not their dancing music, or that the lyrics I knew by heart did not inform their lifestyle.

I liked the idea of the West Side, but where I came from in the 1950's, it might as well have been across the sea in another country instead of just across Central Park, the great divide. Fortunately, through the years I have learned to see life through a larger, more inclusive lens. I have consciously tried to lure the defects of snobbery and arrogant assumptions out of my being, just like the snake charmer who entices the cobra out of the basket. When I moved back to Manhattan in 1984, after living in Massachusetts for nearly fifteen years, I lived on the West Side. I had finally grown past the boundaries of my childhood, but there is a belief in New York that says "Once an East Side girl, always an East Side girl." As hard as I tried to hide my Sutton Place upbringing, anyone who really knows a real "New Yorker" could tell I was an East Side girl.

THE COCKTAIL HOUR

WHEN I WAS TEN, MY father taught me how to make a dry martini. He showed me how to crack the ice, which gin to use (Beefeaters) and how much vermouth to add. He showed me how to pour the gin without bruising it, over the ice and into his favorite old-fashioned glass with the pheasant etched in the crystal. I always put the glass on a small silver tray in case it spilled. He had trained me to bring the martini to him in the living room once he was settled in his faded green, tweed easy chair. I felt very grown up.

My mother sat on the brown couch that was covered with a glazed chintz fabric that had robins and sparrows in flight and ugly plants climbing all over it. Mummy said the fabric had been very expensive and was extremely chic, but I hated it. She always read the *Evening Post*, her tortoiseshell glasses perched on her nose, after she had fixed her scotch on the rocks with a twist. I didn't make scotch cocktails, only martinis.

This was the cocktail hour, a revered family ritual, and nothing whatsoever got in its way. When I was young, I had no idea how traumatic this tradition could be. I can hear my father yelling at my brother to pay attention to the math homework he was trying to help him with, and when I close my eyes I can still see my brother's scrawny shoulders begin to hunch as Daddy grabs the brass poker standing next to the fireplace and shakes it over Lee's trembling body. Lee sobs and runs from the room, leaving me there with my father and his purple-red, angry face. I am terrified too. Where's Mummy? I find her in the kitchen. I tell her about the poker, and that look, that faraway, not present look, comes to her face and she sighs and says, "Oh dear, gin makes your father mean."

There were many nights my parents left our apartment to go to cocktail parties in other people's living rooms. My brother, the family's four-year-old rebel, hated it when they went out. "Don't go," he'd scream, hurling himself on to the hallway floor. I remember one night when he was wearing his Roy Rogers cowboy outfit with the hat and the badge, he lassoed his arms around Daddy's legs, as though he was a rodeo cowboy and Dad was the calf. My father tried to shake the little cowboy free, dragging him across the hall toward the front door. "Get off me," he bellowed, nostrils flaring. "Betty, Betty, where the hell are you? The elevator's coming." Mummy appeared just then, dark green silk swishing around her legs, a dressing drink in her hand and a perturbed look on her face. "Whatever is the matter?"

"Please don't go out," Lee was pleading, whimpering, so pitiful and sad. I was ten, and although I felt sorry for him I was also incredibly embarrassed by this entire display. No one knew what to do, except shut the door and leave. After our parents were gone, our governess Mary retrieved the sheriff's badge that had fallen off Lee's shirt, picked the cowboy hat up off the floor, and told us it was time for bed.

Every Sunday during the year, whether we were in New York or Maine, our family went to my grandparents' for Sunday lunch. Before the meal, everyone sat in the wood-paneled library and William, the butler, mixed noon cocktails. My grandfather, Papa, who had Parkinson's disease, held his glass of scotch with shaking hands, sipping it through a straw as my father happily drank a Manhattan. My grandmother usually ordered a dry vodka martini. I always asked for a Shirley Temple with extra cherries. Wine was not yet included as part of my family's alcohol consumption, so when luncheon was served, the grownups each brought a fresh cocktail to the table.

Sometimes my aunt and uncle spent the weekend at my grandparents' with their young son, my cousin Jay. Jack and Anne lived near Atlantic City in a town called Sweetwater. Their home fit the name. They lived in a modest house beside a river, and there was a small waterfall that became a stream gurgling along a stone trough and flowing into the river. When we went to visit them, Lee and I made little boats and watched them bob along in the stream, always rescuing them from a sure sinking before they sailed into the river. I loved it there. They lived simply, without all the formality that life in Manhattan and my grandparents imposed. Inside the house, there was a cozy dining alcove with a window seat that looked out on the river, and I thought about how different it was compared to my grandparents' dining room, where everyone had to sit up straight and make sure the water in the finger bowls didn't dribble onto the linen placemats.

One particular Sunday lunch when they were visiting, my five-year-old cousin was tired of sitting, so he jumped up and began running around the table. I was horrified and looked at Nanny, whose mouth was tightly pursed, and my father, who fixed a stern eye on my brother, making sure he didn't get up and join Jay in a game of tag. Sunday lunch always took so long, and here was our cousin allowed to get up and be wild.

Lee and I had been sitting at the table watching Helen, the maid, plod around the table holding heavy silver serving platters filled with roast beef and Yorkshire pudding, roast potatoes, and creamed celery. Helen had white hair and wore glasses, just like Papa. She was wearing her formal black uniform with a lace collar and a small white apron, edged with lace. Her thick ankles squeezed out of black lace-up shoes. I was sure she was very uncomfortable and felt sorry for her.

My brother was also uncomfortable. I noticed that he was trying to sit up straight. I knew he was willing his fidgeting body not to slip off the chair to chase Jay. His shoulders were rounded and hunched; they looked like small wings folded over his chest, protecting his heart. Daddy hated it when my brother didn't sit up straight and keep his shoulders back, and he always called attention to his posture at every meal, even in front of everyone at Sunday lunch.

Once, at our own family table, Lee and I were made to sit until we had swallowed all our peas. We kept on chewing, chewing, even when there wasn't enough milk left in the glass to wash the mouthfuls down. I was older, so I had figured out that I could pretend to wipe my mouth with the napkin and deposit the last of the peas into it without being seen. I saw my brother's big brown eyes fill with tears and felt sad for him, but I was impatient because we all had to sit there for a very long time waiting for him to finish. I was terrified when my father began screaming "Swallow your food NOW and put your shoulders back, goddamn it!" I watched as Lee made an effort to push them back by thrusting his chest and chin forward, but after a moment he was caved in again, his head bowed toward his plate.

Not long after one of these frightening incidents, Lee took the hammer and nails that came with a tool bench he had received for Christmas and pounded eight nails into our antique dining room table, the one he had to sit at for so long. He hit every nail so straight and solidly that they disappeared into the polished wood, and I wonder now if each blow of the hammer straightened his shoulders just a little bit.

My anger was displayed in other ways. One afternoon when I came home from school I went into the closet where my mother stored her ballroom dresses in garment bags. Her wedding dress was packed away separately waiting for me to wear someday, but her debutante dress, worn at the Philadelphia Cotillion in 1940, was tucked away safely in the back of one of the bags. It was made of thin tulle, a frothy, feminine, fairy-like fabric. Like a bridal veil. Now and then I'd ask Mummy to take it out and let me try it on.

Of course it was much too large, but I pretended it was perfect, twirling around and curtsying, trying not to trip. Whenever I moved it looked like I was floating in a pale pink and peach cloud.

"Someday you will have a debutante dress of your own," my mother promised me. Now, I pulled the delicate evening gown out of the bag, deciding I would work on it so it would fit and I could be a princess for Halloween. I found a pair of scissors and carefully "hemmed" the dress, cutting a large piece of the bottom off so it would be the right length. I cut the shoestring straps too and pinned them with safety pins. Then I carved out a piece of the midriff, using more pins to hold it in place. Like Mummy, I was not a seamstress. I had asked her to make me a costume, like Stevee's mother had, but she laughed and said, "Oh sweetie, you know I don't sew."

When my mother got home she found me sitting in the middle of pastel tulle. I stood up when she came into the room to show her what I had done. Her gloved hand went to her mouth and a shriek escaped from her mouth. "Oh my God, what have you done to my beautiful dress? Go to your room

this minute. Your father will deal with this when he gets home."
When Daddy "dealt" with things it meant a spanking with the
hand, hairbrush, or belt. Frightened, I waited in my room wondering how bad I had been this time. I always knew, though,
that after Mummy told him what had happened, he'd have a
cocktail "to relax" before coming in to deal with me.

The cocktail hour was a tradition passed on to me, and like
my parents, as I grew to be an adult I took drinking very seriously. Over the years, however, my dependency on Dewar's
Scotch became as strong as the alcohol itself, so I switched to
wine. Jugs of Folonari with screw-off tops were stored in the
pantry, and when my first husband Peter and I lived on Louisburg Square in the late seventies, we placed bottles of aging
French Burgundy and Bordeaux in the wine cellar. When I
look back, some of my best memories were saturated with alcohol. Then, one day six years ago, I knew it was time for me to
stop drinking. Cocktails had turned into multi-faceted, subtle
little drinks of habit and dysfunction, and the wine had taken
on an even greater importance than the scotch I had given up.
Just like my parents' cocktail hour, mine could shift from delightful to ugly in a split second. I could be charming, loving,
and funny; then I might become argumentative, indulgently
emotional, self-centered, and mean-spirited. The ups and
downs began to feel insane, and I finally realized this was not
the way I wanted to live or to be.

Sometimes I feel wistful, especially when I think of all the
wonderful meals that would have been enhanced by a really
good Merlot, and all the Mai Tai fun I have foregone on vacations in Hawaii. But I wouldn't trade my sobriety for those
drinks, not ever. If I did, I'd go back to sleep, instead of waking
to listen to the breeze at dawn.

MAINE

MY HOME IN MAINE IS known as Stonecliff. The driveway into the compound is flanked by stone and wrought-iron gates, and once inside, it forks and leads to the Big House and the Casino, the two houses on the property that look out on the Bay. Visitors drive past well-tended gardens filled with colorful summer annuals: zinnias, snapdragons, dahlias, cosmos, and bright blue bachelor buttons, and at the fork, before it was stolen, they were greeted by a huge bronze toad. I loved that toad. When I was two I began to take responsibility for his nourishment, and every day I scooped up the crushed blue stone gravel from the driveway and deposited it on his head.

I was born in June 1945 a few days after VE Day, and my mother brought me to Maine three weeks later. Daddy was in Europe fighting the Germans. We met when I was three months old. My grandparents had arrived earlier with the servants and the steamer trunks filled with summer clothes, silver, table linens, and various kitchen items from the New York kitchen that Rose, the Irish cook, might need. William, the butler, came with his wife who helped Rose in the kitchen, and Helen, the chambermaid, kept things clean.

Our family inherited the property after Papa, my step-grandfather, passed away from Parkinson's Disease in 1952. Before his illness Papa had been a dynamic business man who, as a child, had grown up in a small coal town in western Pennsylvania, worked his way through college, and later became the president of large utility company. I remember my mother telling me proudly that "your Papa is a self-made man." Mummy was fourteen when she became his stepdaughter, and he adored her, not having a daughter of his own. The father she revered had died two years earlier, and Papa's attention was something she longed for.

Despite the fact that he couldn't move his fingers and had trouble lifting his arms, Papa smoked. His nurse, Mr. Bonner, would light the cigarette and place it carefully between my grandfather's lips. Many days Papa and I played dominoes on the Big House porch, and I watched as his cigarette ash got longer and longer, eventually breaking off and fluttering down onto the dominoes. Then Mr. Bonner got up, removed the cigarette, and tried to dust the ashes off the dominoes without disturbing our game. I also noticed that Papa's lips looked like they hurt. They were dry and cracked, and white spittle formed at the edges of his mouth.

"Give your grandfather a sip of water, Lisa," Mr. Bonner suggested, handing me a glass with a long straw. At five, I felt grown up as I placed the straw in Papa's mouth, making sure it was properly placed, and held it there until he spit it out when he had had enough. I always wondered why he didn't do that with his cigarette. Because it was hard for Papa to speak, when we were not playing a game we sat quietly listening to the seagulls squabble over a clam on the beach, or the hoarse cries of the crows that lived in the tall pine tree next to the house. I'd chatter away like the birds, telling Papa about my plans for the day or making up a story I thought would amuse him. I'd know he was enjoying the story when the right side of his mouth twitched and a tiny lopsided smile appeared.

Then, when I got bored, I would jump up, give my grandfather a kiss on the cheek, and run inside to see what Rose was doing in the kitchen. Once in a while, she would be making her famous chocolate roll and invite me to stay and help her whip the cream and slather the melted chocolate over the cake. The sauce had so much sugar in it that it crunched between my teeth when I licked the spoon. I just loved spending time with "Irish Rose." She was a merry woman who took her cooking very seriously and teased me good naturedly about the fact that I loved to eat. She filled me with food and magical stories of leprechauns who lived at the base of trees in "the old country."

Nanny, who was twenty years younger than Papa, busied herself with keeping Stonecliff running smoothly. In other words, she managed the servants who did all the work. She planned parties and spent time with her friends on the porch of the tennis club, sipping iced tea and watching "the young" play tennis. Although she was only in her fifties, she appeared as and acted like an old lady. I don't remember her doing anything strenuous, like tennis, golf, or even going for walks. She never cooked because that was what Rose did, and the gardening was taken care of by Eddie, the full-time gardener. She wore a hairnet the color of her mousey grey hair whenever there was a slight breeze coming off the bay, and after Papa died she gave away all her pretty colorful dresses and only wore black, navy blue, or grey, the official colors for a widow in mourning. There was an air of sadness about my grandmother, and when I was older I heard the adults whispering that she was drinking in the morning. But at six years old I knew that I was loved by her and that my presence made her happy. Before she became too frightened to leave her apartment in New York, some of my best memories are the times she took me to Broadway musicals and to tea at the Plaza Hotel.

Nanny's name was Mildred, and she grew up outside of Philadelphia. She was the only child of wealthy parents who doted on her. At eighteen, she was named Philadelphia's debutante of the year, and during that year, she met a handsome, dashing young man whose widowed mother, a few years earlier, had left the family farm in Culpepper, VA, and brought her four sons and a daughter to the city. The boys, who were all close in age, had one suit between them that they wore for job interviews. When Mildred married Jamie Emmons, she married out of her "class," and he married "up." They had three children in four years: the youngest, and only, daughter was my mother. Twelve years later, Jamie died of liver cancer at the age of forty-two. With my great-grandfather's help, he had become the owner and president of a coal company, and with his business success created a lifestyle my grandmother was familiar with. On the weekends they left Philadelphia and went to their farm on the Brandywine River, where Jamie had a stable full of race horses and a garage full of foreign cars. He was not a "simple" man, and his expensive tastes, along with the Depression, left his estate $100,000 in debt. So the money was gone for a while. My grandmother sold her home, the cars, and the farm, and she and the children moved in with her parents. A year and a half later, she was married to George, a widower, who, like Mildred and her family, summered in Maine. He had one son who was closer to her in age than George was. After they were married, Mildred and her daughter and two teenage sons moved into his homes in Manhattan and Maine.

Until my brother Lee was born, my parents and I lived with Nanny and Papa in their house we still call "The Big House." The original look, with its weathered grey shingles and single-gabled front, was a simple Maine cottage design, but later, when a large sunroom, kitchen wing, and covered portico entry were added, it became the "Big House." I doubt anyone in my family was aware that our summer home and San Quentin had a name in common.

Life in Maine was a lot less formal than Manhattan, but in both places I grew up surrounded by beautiful material things whose main function was to show off the wealth and privilege of the people to which they belonged. In my grandparents' Manhattan apartment, there were leather-bound books lined up on bookshelves, unread. An English Royal Crown Derby coffee set lay on the antique sideboard in the dining room, unused. Large silver pheasants stood at attention on either side of the English Derby, and when we had a formal Sunday lunch, two pairs of smaller pheasants holding salt and pepper in their plump silver bellies sat at either end of the table. The Big House was not as fancy, but I do remember finger bowls at Sunday lunch, many sets of summer china with engraved flowers around the rims, monogrammed table linens, and perfectly round butter balls that I helped William, the butler, make. I had been taught from a very young age that "living happily ever after" was of the utmost importance, and no matter what, to avoid a "dreary life." Mink, ermine, Steuben Glass crystal, made-to-order English chintz draperies, and twenty-five year-old scotch were thought to be some of the trappings that exempted one from a dreary life. But the most important rule of all was to always look like you were having fun.

Fortunately, it was the natural surroundings of Maine that touched my heart as they crept into my soul, and I waited all winter to come back and be filled with the sounds and smells of Maine. I lay on my bed and listened to the sound of the warm west wind whistle across the water, filling the bay with dancing, frothy white caps and heard the cries of the gulls as they called to one another when they flew past the house. I'd hear the gentle lapping of the bay when it touched the sand on the beach below my bedroom window, and I breathed in its salty tang as it spread through the house like a tasty soup simmering on the stove. I loved the pink scent of wild roses as it entered our house through wooden screen doors, and feeling the summer breeze as it tenderly touched my body. After living for nine months within the grid of New York, where buildings filled the sky, I was soothed by the expansiveness in Maine, where sky and water meet.

Stonecliff was given its name because it was built on ancient stones that don't know or care about privilege or class. As I grew up, I felt the wisdom and strength of those stones and the solid foundation they still represent. Every year the winds and tides change the beach in front of the property, but the rocks remain permanently rooted in place. Their presence has helped me feel anchored and safe. An anchor can keep you secure in a harbor when the seas are stormy and the winds are strong, but it will also keep you from moving and charting a new course. I have often felt the inner winds of my soul blowing me in different directions, urging me to fill the sails and steer myself beyond the protection of my ancestral harbor.

The summer of 1950, after Lee was born, Mummy, Daddy, Lee, and I moved into the Casino, the other house on the property that has always been referred to as "the party house." Nanny had told my parents that Papa was too sick to have children around all the time, especially a tiny baby, and that my parents could fix up the Casino and use it as their summer home.

The house was dark and gloomy. Before we moved in, fur rugs were draped over the balcony, and a large Tiffany lamp hung from a long cord, barely lighting the room below. Instead of colorful wallpaper, like in the Big House, the shingled style house not only had shingles on the outside but on the inside walls as well. Tree trunks held up the beams, and there was one large room downstairs with a small stage at the bay end and a stone fireplace at the other. A balcony ran around the second floor like a gallery and some of the windows were portholes. Visitors still say it reminds them of a boat.

"I hate the Casino, I won't live there," I sobbed when Mummy told me we were moving. "It's scary inside, and there's no kitchen." I moaned, "Why can't we stay in the Big House with Nanny and Papa? Where will we cook? I won't be able to help Rose make chocolate roll."

"Dearie, just wait until you see it in June. You won't recognize it," Mummy replied, trying to reassure me.

And she was right. The next summer when we walked in after the long drive from New York, I fell in love with my new home. During two short weeks in April my parents had gone to Maine to transform the house. They spray-painted the dark wicker chairs and couches white, brightened old tables and a desk with yellow and green paint, and purchased a Victorian style chest that was assigned as The Bar. They added tile and a stall shower in the single bathroom upstairs, and a partition was built downstairs to make space for a tiny kitchen. Our new home had an air of camp to it, and it was ours. The "party house" had become a home.

The forties and fifties were our special "summers on the rocks" when the men, dressed in coats and ties for picnics, brought wicker picnic baskets from Abercrombie and Fitch, complete with silver martini shakers that were balanced precariously on the rocky beach. The summer community came alive in late June, when families from St. Louis, Cincinnati, Philadelphia, New York, and even Memphis, arrived with their steamer trunks and maids. After Labor Day the exodus began and the year-round "natives" reclaimed their community. From

June until early September, the summer people ate lobsters from the local pound, shopped at the small general store, employed many of the year-rounders, and donated money to their community club and church. The relationship between the two groups was, in many ways, symbiotic. Socially, however, it was completely separate. This was pointed out to me when I wanted to play tennis at the small club with Barbara, the daughter of my grandmother's chauffeur David, who was my friend. I was told I couldn't because she wasn't a part of "our circle" and didn't belong to the club. I was furious and confused, but I listened to my grandmother. She made it clear that a friendship with Barbara had restrictions and was not to be taken outside the gates of Stonecliff.

The summer crowd socialized nearly every night, and one year, the widow of one of the summer community's best-known residents had automated carillons installed in the Episcopal chapel on the golf course, in her husband's memory. The bells played familiar hymns every evening at 5:45 PM, and once a friend of my mother's remarked how convenient it was that they went off at that time, "because they call everyone to cocktails."

There were parties every night, and the best parties were the ones given at the Casino.

"Mummy, what are you going to be for the costume party?" I asked her a few days before one of the parties they gave.

"A lobster," she giggled.

"Oh," I answered, wondering how someone who doesn't sew could create such an ambitious costume. "And Daddy, what will he be?"

"He's going to borrow a dress from Rose, wear a blond wig and makeup and go as a woman."

"Oh," I said, confused again, wondering how Daddy could ever look like a woman.

An hour before the party my mother was not looking like a lobster. She had been helping Daddy into his dress, styling his wig, applying his makeup, and trying to squeeze his size ten DDD-width feet into the largest pair of high heels they could find at the Salvation Army Thrift Shop. Every now and then they collapsed into fits of laughter.

"Mummy," I told her impatiently, "you had better get your costume on. The guests will be here soon."

"Oh, my costume has to go on at the very last minute," she replied, winking at Daddy.

After Daddy had been transformed into a funny looking female and went downstairs to get the ice and organize the bar, which was always his job, Mummy pulled her red flannel underwear out of her bottom drawer and put it on. I was thinking she'd be awfully hot and that she was going to need more than red underwear to look like a lobster.

"Where's my hat?" she wondered aloud.

"Is this it?" I answered, spying it on the closet floor.

"Thank you, sweetie, help me put it on."

Then she sat down on the bed and I placed the red cap with red pipe cleaners sticking out of it on her head, being careful to tuck in all her hair because lobsters don't have hair.

"All set," Mummy said. "Let's go downstairs and get the rest of my costume."

As we walked across the upstairs balcony Mummy called down to Daddy, "I'm ready to put it on, Bevy." Daddy disappeared outside on the porch, and when we got downstairs he had come back inside with a lobster trap. The trap was wooden, and Eddie, Nanny's gardener, had made it so that it had a hole large enough to fit a human body instead of a lobster body inside. I was amazed. My mother was going to fit inside and wear a lobster trap! This was very different look from what she wore to parties in New York.

"Lift up your arms, Betty," Daddy suggested. "I have to ease this thing over you very carefully." After much wiggling and shaking and laughing, Mummy was finally entrapped. Her head was sticking out well above the opening, and I noticed that the pipe cleaner feelers on the cap were bent over, so I reached up to straighten them. Thank goodness there were holes for her arms so she could smoke and drink and enjoy her dinner. Lucky she had someone in the kitchen to help with the food. Walking was a little difficult but she managed, and I was sure she would take the trap off later when they rolled up the rugs to dance.

Hours later as the party laughter and chatter competed with Gershwin and Cole Porter tunes on the hi fi and the dancing had begun, I crept out of my room and sat on the balcony, nose pressed against the balustrade, peeking through at the gaiety in the living room below. I loved to watch everyone dance, and I hoped I would have fun like this when I grew up. Just before Daddy spied me and sent me back to bed, I saw my mother dancing a two-step with my friend Helen's father, and I noticed she had taken off her trap.

While my parents were busy with their friends, I spent time with mine, and we never tired of new adventures.

The houses on the bay had sewer pipes that ran down underneath the lawns, onto the beach and into the water. My friends and I noticed that when the tide was especially low the pipe that came out of the Big House didn't quite reach into the water. At age six, we thought it would be interesting to see how long it took the contents of the toilet to make their way through the sewer pipe and onto the beach. So, when Nanny was off with her friends, we assigned someone who had to pee to run up to my grandmother's bathroom to use the toilet, then flush. Those of us left on the beach huddled around the pipe watching closely for whatever had been put into the toilet to come sliding through the pipe and onto the rocks. We were fascinated by this for quite a while, taking turns in the bathroom whether we had to use it or not. Soon we were using leaves, dandelion heads plucked off their stems, and small pieces of paper that we marked with different colored crayons so we could recognize which flush was ours.

From the time I was seven, I was off on my blue Schwinn bike, visiting. We spent a lot of time at the Big Beach, a two-mile sandy beach on the ocean with a small bath house for the summer crowd. When we got tired of swimming and had had enough sun, my friends and I invented the "sneak a peek" sessions at the beach. I had discovered, much to the delight of my girlfriends and me, that there was a peephole in my locker at precisely the same level as "Mr. Older Man's" penis in the locker next door. When we saw him coming up the beach after a swim we rushed to the bath house, waiting for him to come in and change. There were five of us crammed into a space not much larger than a phone booth, giggling hysterically. When "Mr. Older Man," who was a bachelor, finally arrived, we tried to be quiet and focus on the task at hand.

"Let me see," someone whispered much too loudly.

"Give me a turn," giggled another.

"It's *my* locker," I retorted, my right eye pressed up against the hole.

Eventually we tired of this game, or at least of this particular penis, and began to prowl other lockers for other peepholes. Finding none that were as perfectly positioned as the one in locker number four, my friends and I finally gave up this game in favor of others.

I got my first kiss the summer I was eight, from an eleven-year-old boy from Memphis who adored Elvis, wore black, and combed his hair in a pompadour. He had convinced me to ride him home from the village (he sat on the seat while I pedaled as fast as I could) after charging a few comic books from the small summer grocery store. When we arrived at his doorstep, he asked me in to read the comics. No one was home, and after a few moments, he walked over to my chair and planted a kiss on my lips. I was so surprised that I jumped up, pushing the chair over backwards, and ran out the door.

Each summer there was some new game. We played kissing games: dreamboat and spin the bottle. I preferred dreamboat. When it was my turn, I'd lie down on my friend's grandmother's wicker chaise in her sunroom and wait for the boy who drew the shortest end of the stick to come over. I'd stretch out, pucker my lips, trying hard to look like Marilyn Monroe, and wait for my "dreamboat" to bend over and give me a kiss.

The summer I was nine my twelve-year-old friend Eleanor invited me to play strip poker with her and some of her older friends. "Wear plenty of clothes," she advised. I arrived in two pairs of shorts, three tee shirts, three pairs of socks and four pairs of underpants. I also borrowed twelve bobby pins from Mummy's drawer and stuck them in my hair. Needless to say, I didn't "lose."

When I was eleven I got teased for having breasts and an especially large big toe. I refused to wear a bra because I was so self-conscious, but Mummy was right when she told me that wearing only an undershirt would cause more attention. I flopped around the tennis court, jiggling every time I ran.

I hated wearing shoes, and one day the boys in my group noticed my big toe:

"Wow, look at that toe, it's as big as two of mine put together. It looks like a barge." They dubbed it The Barstow Big

Toe, and I suppose I should have felt some pride in the fact that no one had one like it. It had a squareness and girth that everyone thought remarkable, but I hated it. Just like the thin body I was expected to have and was constantly wishing for, I wanted a slim, sophisticated toe. A feminine toe that didn't call attention to itself, like the way I was raised.

I remember Mummy clicking her tongue in disapproval at Saks Fifth Avenue when we were buying shoes for dancing school.

"I can't believe that you need a triple D width shoe. You've inherited your father's wide feet," she'd sigh.

But I knew better. I needed wide shoes because of my toe. Once, Nanny bought me a pair of alligator pumps with ankle straps and a small bow at the top of the shoe. I wanted those shoes so badly that I tried to ignore the way they made me hobble around because the style just didn't fit my foot.

"I don't understand why your grandmother bought you those shoes," Mummy said when she noticed I was limping. "You obviously don't have the kind of feet that can wear that kind of shoe." I was horrified when I realized that my feet were more like the ugly stepsisters' than Cinderella's. There would be no glass slipper for me, and I'd probably never get a prince because of my wretched, oversized big toe.

By the end of each summer, I was a little wild. I hated leaving the freedom of Maine and sobbed on and off during the drive back to Manhattan. But it wasn't just the freedom I would miss; I was leaving the fresh air and the golden afternoon light, the tranquil blue bay and the seagulls who perched on the rocks down on the beach. I'd miss my brother's shining brown eyes, Mummy's relaxed, tan face, and Daddy's bleached blond hair, his easy grin. It seemed on the surface we were all happier in Maine.

SHATTERING

I CAN HEAR THE BREEZES dance through the wind chimes on the deck and when I close my eyes I am seven again, back in my bedroom in Maine, listening to the swaying sound of the bell buoy in the bay. My buoy, my bay, my child Lisa listening as I lie curled up, knees to chest, hand on heart, listening and watching gulls gently soaring on the west wind that whistles through the shingles of my home.

I strain my ears to hear other sounds downstairs. There are sounds of laughter and ice clinking into glasses, ice shattering into pieces like a broken mirror as the cracker comes down hard, and fills the short, scotch on the rocks, glass. Now I hear the amber sound of whiskey cascading over the pieces of ice. Laughter, shattering ice, gulls mewing, the bell buoy.

Mummy's laugh is forced. She really doesn't think Daddy is very funny. How do I know? I just do. I think Daddy is funny and so I always laugh because I want to please him. I take care of Daddy. What else can I do? Mummy tries, but he loves me more. I don't think she knows he loves me more. I am his good girl. I fill their holes, and they aren't rabbit holes. Rabbit holes are filled with mystery and magic. The holes I fill are full of tears and rage and unexpressed dreams.

Yes, I am an eight-year-old shining princess with a wand called "Fix It." I think that I should be the knight on the white charger, but I prefer to be a princess in a sparkly sequined gown with a diamond crown. Oh, but truly I am a warrior who doesn't know she is a little girl. The little girl is curled up in her bed listening to the sounds on the bay.

I lived split between being an innocent, happy child and one whose innocence was shattered because I could feel the insides of people. I was a child who believed she could make her parents happy if she could shine brightly enough. Later on in my life, I yearned for wholeness, for the laughter to be real. I crawled on my knees toward the round door of wholeness. I heard God say: "Don't go back to sleep, little Lisa. I am here with you now. You do not have to fill their holes, or anyone else's. Step inside your own circle and watch your own life float by.

Now I am on my back in the tranquil bay, looking up at the sky that wraps me in blues and greys. I can see storm clouds forming but I still lie there, floating peacefully in my life. No need to leave this place of serenity and peace. They have been inside me all along. I know that God holds me there, even when I forget to ask Him. He will hold me even when the shattering begins.

DISEASE

SOME MORNINGS IN NEW YORK, I would go into my parents' bedroom to say goodbye before leaving for school. Mummy was usually still sleeping soundly, but Daddy was often awake, propped up slightly on his pillows, smoking a cigarette.

On this particular day the shades and blue toile curtains are still drawn so it is very dark in the room. I can barely see Daddy, but I can smell the smoke from his cigarette and know he is awake. An ashtray full of stale cigarette butts and a half-empty glass of scotch are sitting on the night table next to his bed, and I scrunch up my nose, the way you do when you don't like how something smells.

"Want me to open the curtains, Daddy?" I ask. "It's a beautiful sunny day."

"Good God no," he yells at me. "I've got a migraine."

"Can I get you some aspirin?"

"No, I've already had some. This will pass."

"What can I do then, Daddy?"

"Nothing, little girl, nothing," he replies, trying to give me an encouraging smile.

I look over at Mummy and notice that she is wearing the white cotton gloves she uses to keep from scratching her eczema in the night. She has to tie them to her wrists with string, or else she would tear them off in her sleep when the itching gets really bad. She must have had a bad night, I think to myself, because there are slender streaks and dots of blood all over the gloves. I hate the eczema. It covers her body and makes her skin look angry and sick. The itching and inflammation always distract her and compete for my time.

I had begun to worry a lot about my parents. I could see the eczema on Mummy and I knew that Daddy's head hurt when he got migraines, but what really scared me was the cancer that moved into our family when my parents were in their mid-thirties.

The same year that Daddy taught me how to make a martini, I learned about cancer. I was ten when after a biopsy, my father was told there was a malignancy in the bone around his right eye and that both the bone and his eye would have to be removed.

"There will be a hole instead of an eye and I will have to wear a black patch," Daddy explained. "I'll look like a pirate," he added with a fake brave smile. When he came home from the hospital after the surgery he looked really scared and was in a lot more pain than he felt during a migraine. The place where his eye had been was covered with a large bandage that needed changing every day. Underneath the bandage a thick wad of gauze was stuffed into the bloody hole. I wasn't prepared for the blood, or that one of my Daddy's nice green eyes had been plucked out.

Within a year after my father's wound had healed my mother found a lump on her right breast. After a radical mastectomy she came home from the hospital, and there were more bandages and more blood. Sometimes when she was taking her bath I would sit on the toilet seat and look at her ugly scar. Instead of a small soft breast there was an angry red wound. I remember thinking how lonely her other breast looked. I felt lonely too. I had no one to talk to about the cancer that was bringing fear and chaos into our family. We were all afraid of it but we didn't know how to talk about our fears. Mummy believed in "rising above it," and I wanted to but I couldn't. I didn't know where I fit in this cancer world. None of us did.

I had seen more of the disease than just my parents' cancer. My paternal grandmother Gommy volunteered at the James Ewing Hospital, a public cancer clinic that was part of Memorial Sloan-Kettering, and I would go with her at Christmastime to see the patients and hand out gifts. Many of them had unusual malignancies, cancers that had eaten their noses, ears, and jaws. This disease called cancer terrified me because I knew it had eaten a part of my mother and father too.

It was during this time that food became an endless source of comfort to me. Perhaps I thought that if I ate enough, then cancer wouldn't come and eat me too. I had always loved food, and I'd happily eat anything except for brussels sprouts and okra. I even liked calves' liver and tongue, which were served regularly at our dinner table. Food was always there for me. It was becoming my best friend. I didn't want to look thin and emaciated like the cancer patients at the hospital, but I didn't want to get fat either. That would displease Mummy and shame the family. Daddy got fat when he ate or drank too much, and Mummy would moan if the scale went to 120 pounds. (She was 5'6" tall.) She was very critical of Daddy or me when we put weight on, and I believe now that she worried if anyone in our family was fat, it would "look" to her friends as though something was wrong. How could she think people wouldn't notice that something was wrong? My father's eye was missing, and her breast had been cut away. I guess the emotional "stiff upper lip" approach created an illusion of wholeness.

I hurt for my parents, I hurt for my brother, and I didn't understand then that the person I hurt the most for was me. Instead of seeing or feeling it, I drugged myself with food.

I snuck food at night sometimes when everyone was sleep-

ing, and during the day I bargained for it at school. At recess
lunch we were served sandwich halves and milk, and every day
during a class before our snack, I would pass notes to my friends
who didn't care much about food, asking them if they wanted
their sandwich half or not. Sometimes I'd have a good day and
end up with my half and three others.

When I was nine I ate the entire box of Valentine candy
my parents had given me and threw up the chocolates all over
the Monopoly game my brother and I were playing. When I
received one of those little electric ovens that came with the
ingredients for baking, I tasted the mix and loved it so much
that I ate it raw before it had a chance to make it into the oven
and become a cake.

That same year, I took on a standing rib roast. My parents
were having a dinner party, and after everyone was served,
Mummy took the roast back into the kitchen to cover it with
tin foil and keep it warm, in case her guests wanted second
helpings. Smelling the meat cooking all afternoon and watching Daddy carve it in the pantry had made me ravenous, even
though I had eaten my dinner earlier. I never thought about
the eight people in the dining room when I went into the
kitchen, picked up the knife and proceeded to gouge the beef.
I went in knife point first, intent on getting to what I knew to
be the choicest, most tender parts. When I had finished the
roast had no core. It was still able to stand on its own but its
inside was missing. I had eaten its center.

Food addiction goes to the core, and it will eat your
center.

As the years went by the diseases and dysfunctional conditions in my family created a ripe environment for deepening
my emotional hole. A bottomless pit of fear was forming inside
that could only be satiated by food.

DANCE

WE HAD AIR RAID DRILLS at my private all-girls' school. Several times a year, the siren went off and grades one through six (the older girls went somewhere else underground) filed down the stairs to the basement and lined up in a room called the Holland Tunnel, named, I suppose, for one of the two tunnels that connect New York with New Jersey. The teachers lined us up in rows and told us to sit down, while they checked the dog tags that we had to wear every day. The dog tags had tiny raised bumps on them that spelled out our name and address and were attached to our necks by an ugly chain. Mostly, I forgot about mine since it was stuffed out of sight under my uniform, but one time during the drill I asked my second grade teacher why we had to wear dog tags, and she told me, "Well, Lisa, if the Russians drop the bomb on New York and we were blown up and weren't recognizable, the police would need to identify our bodies, wouldn't they?"

During the 1950's the Holland Tunnel was the school's bomb shelter, and it was also the room where I took dance class every week. Miss Heny, our teacher, looked like a gypsy. She wore a dark red scarf around her head and had large hoop earrings. Her eyes and nose were sharp, like an eagle's, and she had the skinniest body I had ever seen. She moved through the room like a cat, soft and agile, and even though she was different from the other teachers, and very strict, I absolutely loved her class.

We would take off our pale green tunics and dance in white blouses and green bloomers, and instead of our sturdy brown Oxfords we wore sandals made of soft suede. When Miss Heny put the music on and began to move her body through the room, telling us to follow her, I lost all fear of her as I tried to imitate her graceful movements. I leaped and twirled, bending my body to the rhythm of the music that filled the room. But what really transformed us from a line of "little ladies" into free floating forms of movement were the scarves. Miss Heny had a bag of scarves, and at some point during class she would take the drawstring bag from the shelf, open it, and shake a rainbow of soft silk colors onto the hard linoleum floor.

They were beautiful, like flowers, with a dozen different colors blending together waiting to be picked. In one particular class I chose the pale pink scarf and announced that I was going to be a butterfly and dance amongst the flowers. I closed my eyes and felt the music float inside my body, imagining that my arms were wings and I could really fly. The scarf became part of my body too, and for a few sacred moments I became a butterfly. I moved gracefully and softly through the same room where earlier I had sat on the floor during the air raid drill, my dog tag around my neck, frightened of the bomb and imagining my mutilated body not ever moving again.

When I was five I began going to dancing school to learn ballroom dancing. Instead of scarves and soft sandals I wore white gloves and black patent leather shoes. My dresses were organdy and above the knee, and on special occasions I was allowed to wear the antique lace dresses my grandmother had brought back from Paris before the war. The boys wore navy suits with short pants until they were eight or nine. In Manhattan's aristocratic circle the rules of the British royal family were followed. The Queen's son Prince Charles wore short pants, and so the sons of my mother's social circle did also.

Mummy and I took a cab to a club on Park Avenue that had a large ballroom with a parquet wooden floor, crystal chandeliers, and delicate gold painted chairs arranged in a large circle. The boys and girls waited in a smaller room before marching into the ballroom. The girls stood in a tight cluster, like geese, chattering away with each other. We were well aware that we were being closely watched and considered as partners by the boys, who, even after several years of practice, still looked quite nervous and out of place. I guess it took until you were at least eleven or twelve to get the social etiquette down pat, even though we Manhattan children had been watching our parents model the decorum of "high society" manners for years. I almost never got chosen by a boy and certainly never by a boy I liked, so I usually ended up marching in at the back of the line with a girl, because the girls without boy partners always went last.

Once in the ballroom, we had to shake hands and curtsy or bow to the dancing school instructor. He was elegantly dressed in a navy double-breasted suit and shiny black shoes. He had a tiny moustache like Clark Gable. His dancing partner, Miss Vera, who Mummy said was *more* than just his dancing partner, stood beside him. She had excellent posture and wore satin dresses with full skirts that swayed and billowed while they demonstrated a dance. When I was finally in the middle of the room and had curtsied as though Miss Vera was the Queen, I'd walk quickly to the side of the room and sit down on one of the gold chairs that didn't look like it would hold anyone heavier than the smallest girl. I thought everyone was looking at me and wished I could stuff my body under one of the chairs. I wasn't as pretty as Maggie or as thin as Mazie, and I hated it when the boys cut in on them and never on me.

Mummy sat in the gallery at the end of the ballroom with the other mothers, watching us dance by. If I was looking unhappy because I was dancing with a boy who came up to my armpit, and who I thought was the ugliest, fattest boy in the entire room, she'd catch my eye and pull her mouth up into a smiling position with two fingers. Later she reminded me: "Sweetie, you must always look like you are having a good time even when you're not."

I suppose my love of dancing came from my parents, Betty and Bev. Their friends said that when they danced together they were as graceful as Fred Astaire and Ginger Rogers. I always loved the story about them dancing over chairs and sofas at a party in Maine.

Mummy wasn't Daddy's only partner. I danced with him too. As I grew older, we did a mean two-step and jitterbug at the Club's summer dances, and I loved it when people watched us because we danced so well together. My friends told me that my father was as handsome as a movie star. They thought he looked just like Tab Hunter. But my father was not a slim man, like Cary Grant or Gregory Peck, my mother's favorite actors. He had an athletic build that was heavy set and stocky. I hated hearing my mother and grandmother mention, with looks of visible dismay, what a shame it was that I had been born with my father's physique, instead of Mummy's slender frame. What

I hated even more was the remark a friend of my mother's gave me when I was five: "Oh Betty," she said one day. "Lisa is square! Look at her hands and her feet. There is nothing long about her, even her bangs are chopped short. I'm going to call her 'the square child.'"

When I danced in front of the mirror in our living room to the music of Cole Porter and Gershwin, singing along with Ella, I'd forget that I wasn't as slim as the *Vogue* models my mother admired. I became as graceful and elegant as Cyd Charisse when she danced with Gene Kelly in *An American in Paris*. Everything I didn't want to think about fell away when I took flight across the room.

I have a picture of myself at eighteen. I am sitting on the floor at my father's apartment wearing a blue flowered-print dress. Its full skirt surrounds me like a still blue pond. My legs are folded under my body, and I wonder now if I imagined for a moment that I looked as delicate and graceful as a swan floating on the pond. Daddy is sitting on the couch, and he looks so different than the father who swirled me around the dance floor at my debutante party a few months earlier. I notice how thin he is and that his face is drawn and grey. He is only forty-three, but for the first time he looks older than his age. When I lean over to give him a kiss, he winces.

"I'm sorry Lisa," he says in a hoarse whisper, "but every time I move, my side feels like there are sharp knives going into it. The pain killers aren't working as well as they used to."

"Oh Daddy, I am so sorry. I wish that there was something I could do." I am so frightened. His cancer has returned, and I know there isn't anything I can do to ease his pain. It is horrible—unthinkable—to see my father in so much pain.

"Lisa, there is something you can do. I want you to dance for me."

I immediately feel embarrassed. "Oh Daddy, can't you dance with me? We'll go slowly."

"No sweetie, it hurts too much. Let me sit here and watch. You dance alone this time." He hands me a record that is on the table next to him. "Put this record on, it's one of your favorites." I stand up and go over to the record player to put the record on: it flips down, the needle swings over, and there's Ella again, singing "In the Still of the Night." I hesitate.

"Dance," Daddy demands. "Forget about me."

I begin to move slowly at first, feeling stiff, self-conscious. Then the rhythm picks up, and I begin to twirl, bending my body to the music. I am moving faster now, no longer confined to the living room. Like a bird, I have taken off, dancing into the bedroom, through the living room again, and into the dining room. I am in my body and losing it at the same time. I breathe hard, my heart pumping in my chest. Happy and alive, I stretch my arms out like the branches of a large and graceful tree. I become the wind blowing through the tree, and as my bird spreads her wings, I soar on the wind. I am completely caught up in myself as I dance for my father. As Ella croons the words "will this dream of mine fade out of sight . . . ?" I begin to sing with her. I twirl past Daddy, who is singing along with me. He looks happy and sad all at the same time, and I feel beautiful as I dance for him.

It was fifty-five years ago I danced for my father. I am so glad that I did not sit that dance out. I still feel the exhilarating joy when I open my arms and move my body through air, feet trying to let go of the earth. Dancing brings me into myself and dislodges the parts of me that I have allowed to build walls, like sandcastles, over which I cannot see. I dream now of the beach and tell my child to let herself go. Instead of my father's living room, I am on the wet sand, commanding myself to *DANCE child, rub yourself with sand; coat it on your body. Now, move into the waves, become the surf. Not the gentle water that lingers at the end of the wave, but the rolling frenzy of the wave that knows its power that creates new form on the beach. Creating new form is what movement can do. Dance is like the wave that brings the sandcastles. down.*

THE DANCE OF FORGIVENESS

MY EYES OPEN SUDDENLY. I am lying on my back on my bed in Maine. I never sleep on my back. It is as if I have come out of a trance, not sleep. It is 3:00 AM and the date is July 17, 1973, eight years to the day my father died. I remember in vivid detail what I have come to believe was a visitation, not a dream. My father's soul, connecting across dimensions, danced with mine on the lawn in front of our house by the bay.

I can still feel it today, thirty-five years later. The moment carved outside of real time; a dying man's request, not able to be spoken before his last breath, and the soul, given a second chance to be set free. All I could think of when my eyes opened was that I had been with my father and something had been made right. We had danced our last dance.

I am walking between the Casino and the Big House. The lilac bushes crowd the path so that I have to duck under them. There is just enough light from an ascending half moon to guide me. Then I see him. He is stretched out on the stone path, his body lying in a pool of blood.

"Daddy, oh my God, Daddy, you are covered in blood. What are you doing here? Why is there so much blood? You died of cancer, there wasn't any blood." He reaches his arms out toward me, and I grab hold of his hand to help him sit up. There is bright, red blood everywhere.

"Please forgive me, Lisa" he cries. "Forgive me."

"Of course I forgive you, I answer him. I forgave you a long time ago Daddy." Then he smiles a radiant smile and gets to his feet. "Dance with me then." He takes me in his arms and we dance out onto the lawn, waltzing in circles, away from the bloodied path. We are transformed by the joy of movement, lit up by the light of the moon. Then our dance begins to slow down, he lets go of me, falls onto the grass and dies, a gentle, peaceful smile on his face.

My eyes open. I am lying on my back on my bed.

Was this my father's resurrection?

Yesterday I was reading a passage from Hebrews in the Old Testament of the Bible that says, *Without the shedding of blood, there is no forgiveness.* The discipleship book I am studying then stated, *That is why God sent Jesus who was without sin to shed His blood upon the cross for the forgiveness of our sins.*

It is Holy Week 2008, and I have just walked across the doorsill where the two worlds touch.

BEV

MY FATHER WAS FORTY-FOUR WHEN he died, and I have often wondered if the cancer that claimed his eye was his body's way of telling him there were things he didn't see. When I think of him, dying so young without the generosity of time to see himself more clearly, I feel renewed compassion for this man. When the cancer spread to his lungs was it telling him he couldn't breathe under the weight of all that stress? Too much gin, too many lies, betrayal, and guilt is a lot to breathe through and survive.

I wanted to save him, but I was just a child.

Unless I asked him, he didn't talk about the war where he shot at Germans from an armored tank. I pled with him to tell me the stories of the near misses he had, and about the medal he won that was encased in a paperweight on his desk.

"Oh," he'd sigh, "I was in a foxhole with some of the men, and there was a line of Germans heading toward us. The soldier next to me had a grenade in his hand, and when he pulled the pin he froze. He couldn't throw the grenade. I realized that if that grenade went off in the foxhole we would all be killed, instead of the Germans; so I knocked the grenade out of his hand and threw it myself. It was a close call."

The story my mother told me about the war was that Daddy had an affair with a French woman while he was overseas. She told me that she had found a letter he wrote to this woman before he had sent it. It explained that the promises he had made to her couldn't be kept. He had a baby daughter now, and he would not be coming back to France to be with her. There was no medal for that close call.

There were other affairs, and after nineteen years of marriage one of them turned into something more and my father left our home. Three years earlier, when I was twelve, I found an Easter card that told the truth about my parents' marriage.

It is a beautiful Easter Sunday in 1958. The service we have just attended is at the church Mummy and Daddy were married in fifteen years ago, the church we go to every Sunday as a family. After wishing all our friends a Happy Easter on the steps of the church, I suggest to my parents that we walk down Fifth Avenue for a while.

"I want to see the fancy hats and dresses, be a part of the Easter Parade," I tell them. I notice there are Easter lilies planted on the Park Avenue "islands" where the trees at Christmas had been, and I can smell their sweet spring scent when the wind blows in my direction.

But Daddy is in a hurry to get home, and he whistles for a cab before we have even walked a block. He sits in the front seat chatting with the driver, while in the back seat Lee rolls the window up and down, cranking the handle incessantly. Finally, my father turns around, and glaring at him tells him to knock it off. Mummy is sitting quietly, staring out the window. I am wedged between her and my brother, and now and then she looks over at me and tells me to get my hair out of my eyes.

My grandmother Nanny had died a month earlier, and I am very sad that we aren't going up to Nanny's for Easter lunch. Her servants and my friends, Rose, William, Helen, and Agnes, have left and taken new jobs, and my grandmother's beautiful apartment had just been sold. My aunts and uncles and cousins are visiting somewhere else, so it is just going to be the four of us for Easter dinner.

Mummy and Daddy are in the kitchen mixing a cocktail and preparing our traditional Easter meal: leg of lamb, new potatoes, and asparagus with hollandaise sauce. Mummy is a good cook, but she doesn't bake, so for dessert she bought a cake shaped like an Easter egg with pastel icing laced and swirled in pretty designs all over it. It looks delicious, but I miss Rose's homemade desserts and wonder what she is making for the new people she works for. My brother has gone into his room to play by himself, and after a few minutes in the kitchen I decide to go into my parents' bedroom and watch some T.V. Nothing much is on, just a few church services, so I turn it off and walk over to Daddy's bureau to look at myself in the mirror.

Then I see the card. It has two yellow ducks sitting by a pond with several ducklings nestled around them. Beside the pond there is a spring-green willow tree, and the words "Easter is a time of hope" are written just above the scene. Curious, I open the card and see Mummy's handwriting. I begin to read:

"*I know that you don't love me anymore. . . .*"

"*For the sake of the children, please don't leave. . . .*"

"*Give me another chance, I'll change. . . .*"

It is signed: "*I love you, Betty.*"

I feel like I have just been swallowed by something huge and invisible and there is no one to help get me out so that everything will be all right again. I am dazed and dizzy and sit down on Daddy's bed. I read the card again. It is like trying to interpret a foreign language. It doesn't make any sense. My heart is pounding, and the terror I feel is working itself into a hard fist. When the fist gets too big inside to bear I stand up and leave the bedroom with the card in my hand. I walk into the pantry and Daddy looks up from the bar. He has a few cubes of ice in one hand and is smashing them with an ice breaker.

"What is this? What does this mean?" I shake the card at Daddy, feeling some relief because the fist is opening and becoming the tears that are streaming down my cheeks. Daddy looks frightened.

"Tell me why you wrote this, Mummy." I am beginning to raise my voice as I walk into the kitchen where she is making the hollandaise. The top of her red and white checked apron has come untied, and her pretty lavender cashmere sweater has a few flecks of bright yellow egg yolk on it. Her face looks so tired. The lines that frame her mouth are like deep scars carved around it. She sees me holding the card and her shoulders slump. She bows her head over the pot. She doesn't stop stirring.

"You'd better handle this, Bev," is all she says.

Then it gets very quiet. No one seems to be breathing. All I hear is the spoon rubbing against the sides of the pot, and from his bedroom, I can hear Lee happily singing the Davy Crockett song: "Born on a mountain top in Tennessee. . . ." I wonder if he is wearing his coonskin hat.

"Come into the bedroom," Daddy says, interrupting my thoughts. We leave Mummy in the kitchen, taking the card into their room. Daddy closes the door and sits down in the desk chair, as I perch myself across from him on the edge of the chaise lounge. I listen to the cars and buses on Sutton Place, and I wonder how there could be ordinary, everyday sounds coming through the window when it feels like my world has become so completely surreal.

I watch Daddy's face. Since his cancer surgery it seems as though he cries more, like when we watch *Father Knows Best* on T.V., and whenever he does, I imagine that the tears flow out of his real eye into the hole under his patch. When the hole fills up, he has to remove the patch and rub the place where his other eye used to be. He is doing that now. He is rubbing the hole. For a moment he doesn't look at me, he just rubs and rubs.

I break the silence. "Why don't you love Mummy anymore? How can that be true? People who are married always love each other, don't they, don't they Daddy?" I am gulping for air as my sobs fill my body, but I have to keep talking. "Are you going to leave us? Please don't leave us." I am begging him.

After a moment he looks at me and says, "I don't expect you to understand, you're too young. Your mother is a wonderful woman and I respect her very much, but it is true, I am not in love with her anymore."

"But you can't leave," I insist. "You won't." My tone sounds like a command instead of a plea.

Daddy hesitates. His head is down, and I can tell he is thinking hard. He finally looks up at me and says, "Now that you know the truth I won't leave. Mummy and I will see what we can do to make things better. Let's try and forget about the card and have a nice Easter dinner." Then he stands up and leaves the room.

I sit alone staring out the window. I keep hearing the words "Daddy doesn't love Mummy anymore" repeating themselves over and over in my head. Later that evening when my parents are watching T.V. in their bedroom I sneak out to the kitchen and eat the rest of the Easter egg cake. I want to forget about the card.

But of course I didn't forget. I spent the next three years acutely aware of how my parents interacted with one another. I watched their body language with the vigilance of a hawk looking for nourishment, and I listened intently for words of endearment that might pass between them. Any sign that Daddy loved Mummy again.

My father might not have known how to be faithful to my mother, but he did know how to discipline his children. He had learned well. Daddy's father died when Daddy was a year old, and after being brought up by nannies, my grandmother sent him to boarding school when he was twelve. The teachers used wooden paddles on the students when they needed to be re-minded about inappropriate conduct. They formed two lines, and when it was my father's turn, he would be made to crawl between them on his hands and knees, pants down, as they took their shots at his behind. Daddy always laughed when he told this story, but I didn't think it was very funny. He had used the bare-bottom spanking too often with me.

I should think that rage turned inward has to leak out somehow. The yelling, the gin, hot ego, spreading like a wildfire out of control, and the cancer at thirty-four, bringing him to a decision to try and find happiness while he still had time. When Daddy did leave in 1961, my mother was gracious enough to observe that when someone faces the possibility of dying, that person reassesses his or her life. Grasping for more pleasure, people often make rash changes.

I wonder now if a life in chaos can ever be lived consciously. I know that active alcoholism will keep the spirit detached and the mind in turmoil, and that fear is the fuel that ignites despair from the deepest place within. My father, in his escape from reality, turned away from himself and, I believe, from God. He tried to numb so many feelings with two martini lunches and drinks before and after dinner, that when the cancer came he had little choice but to be consumed by the demons pursuing him. A man living in his center stands his ground and takes them on, like a warrior.

Recalling the happy memories is just as important as remembering the sad ones, and fortunately, I have found while writing this book that the good ones hold as much clarity as the ones that have caused me pain. I remember Mummy telling me a delightful story when I was nine or ten, and I have always imagined it as one of the times she and Daddy were happiest during their marriage.

A year or so after their 1942 wedding they went to live at Fort Riley, in Kansas. Daddy's superb horsemanship, learned as a young boy, had made him eligible to be in the Cavalry branch of the Army, and he was sent to Fort Riley to teach soldiers how to ride. When it came time for him to go overseas, flesh-and-blood horses were replaced by steel armored tanks to ride into battle.

"It was such fun at Fort Riley," Mummy told me one day when we were taking our basset hound Timmy for a walk. "While your father was busy teaching and being trained I met so many interesting people."

"Like who, Mummy?" I questioned.

"Oh, the actress Jean Tierney became a friend of mine, and the dress designer Oleg Cassini was there also." These names didn't impress me as much as Les Barker, whom I knew because he became Tarzan in the movies after the war.

"You knew Tarzan?" I asked her.

"Well, yes. But we didn't know him like that then. He was a good-looking guy but nothing special." Then she laughed. "Of course no one had seen him in a loin cloth yet! I know it sounds strange, with the war going on, but that year out in Kansas felt carefree," Mummy continued. "It was the first and only time Daddy and I were on our own, away from our family, in a place that was so different from everything we had known. The war in Europe was a dreadful nightmare, but we didn't believe our men would be shipped overseas, so we didn't worry about their safety. Daddy was riding horses, something that he loved, and I was making friends with people I would never have met otherwise. We really did have a good time. Sometimes too much of a good time," she added with one of her mischievous smiles. Timmy had peed a few times, and I was worried that Mummy would start toward home and the conversation would end.

"What do you mean? Tell me a story," I pressed her, heading the dog in the direction of the park.

"Well, one night the officers and their wives were in the mess hall having dinner. The women were dressed quite formally, and the men were in uniform, of course. The food was so good out there you could hardly believe it was Army cuisine. On that particular night the meal was especially good because rumor had it that the general and his wife were going to be there for dinner. We had finished the main course and they hadn't arrived yet, so we all assumed they wouldn't be coming. Then the cream puffs were brought out on large trays from the kitchen and one was placed in front of each person. I have no idea who started it, but it certainly wasn't your father. All of a sudden the dining room became a battle zone. Cream puffs were hurtling through the air like small grenades, whipped cream was exploding everywhere, and some of the men had begun to help themselves to more 'ammunition' off the trays. Everyone was shrieking with laughter." She paused then, for the effect, I imagine.

"What happened then? Tell me, Mummy," I was desperate to know.

"Just as the food fight was at its peak, who should arrive but the general and his wife."

"Oh no!" I was truly horrified. "What did you do?"

"Well, Daddy was one of the lucky ones. He had seen his commanding officer coming just before he was about to throw another cream puff and jumped out the window. It was convenient that the mess hall was on the first floor and the windows were level with the ground. Actually quite a few of the men got out that way, but the ones caught were severely reprimanded by the general."

"What does that mean?" I asked as we turned the corner just a block away from home.

"That means they were punished for not acting with the appropriate conduct expected of officers in the United States Army," she said with a little flourish. "Like when you have bad table manners or spill your milk and you are sent to your room."

I wasn't sure, but it seemed as though a cream puff food fight was much worse than spilling milk, especially when it was an accident. But I did understand just how important table manners were in our family, and Daddy, like the general, always got to decide what was appropriate and what wasn't.

I know now that all the memories we hold inside make up the story of our lives, and that no experience can ever be deleted from the whole. Life is always changing, but nothing that has been lived can ever be completely lost. When I want to feel the texture of my memories about my father, whether they are happy or sad, I feel my mind in my body and remember. Here are a few scenes:

There's Daddy doubled over laughing at my brother who is acting like a clown, and I hear him say, "Lee, you'll be in the theater someday."

Daddy really angry and sending Lee and I to our rooms because we switched the salt for the sugar: "April Fools!"

His tuxedo hanging outside his bedroom window to dry after a night of hard dancing at the 4th of July dance in Maine.

Daddy leaving the apartment with his suitcase. The sounds of the heavy metal door slamming shut and Mummy sobbing in her room.

Daddy with cancer again; vulnerable, frightened, softer, sweet. Acting like the man I always knew that he was.

BETTY

MY MOTHER'S LINEN DRESS HAS been hanging in her bedroom closet for thirty-five years. It is two-tone, grey, and pale blue with a tiny bit of beige at the waist, a dress she would have worn to cocktails or church, not dressy enough for dinner. I can see her now: beige patent leather shoes, panty hose (even in the summer) and a cream-colored cashmere sweater draped around her shoulders. Her thin hair, always such a disappointment to her, is curled, teased, and blanketed with extra spray whose sole function is to battle the humidity.

The dress still looks quite fresh. However, owing to the mustiness of a Maine closet, it lost her smell, Shalimar, years ago. It's a size eight, and a few years ago when I was thin enough to wear it, I realized that it was too late. It wasn't my style. I tried to look like my mother until I was nearly forty. She died before my twenty-seventh birthday. Perhaps trying to look like her was one of the ways I kept her alive. Her summer friends would tell me: "Oh my dear, you look so much like Betty. How I loved your mother. She died much too young. How old was she, I've forgotten?"

"She was just fifty," I'd reply, then add, "Yes, she was much too young."

I remember the last day I looked like her. It was Easter Sunday 1985, and I was wearing Laura Ashley. My hair was curled and styled, and I wore red Pappagallo shoes to match my dress. I had Adrian, my four-year-old son, dressed like an English boy, the way my mother had dressed my brother Lee: navy blue shorts, a white shirt, knee socks, and Oxfords. I had moved back to Manhattan the year before and was living on Central Park West. Adrian, my brother, his son Taylor, and I were rowing on the frog pond in Central Park. I didn't look very West Side, even in 1985, and I knew that my WASPY East Side roots were showing.

It was around this time that I decided I wanted to look like me, but I had no idea what that was. I was tired of the style "rules" of my past and of worrying what other people would think if I was different. I not only wanted to look like me but I wanted to act like me as well. Thanks to a training in body-mind therapy and my own personal therapy sessions, I began to explore my past and observe the self I had become. As Rumi writes, "the door is round and open," but you have to be willing to walk through it. I believe God wanted me to cross through and begin the search for my own identity. I gave myself permission to leave my ancestors at *their* round and open doors and go find my own portal. Please do not think I am saying God cares whether I wear Laura Ashley or jeans and an embroidered Indian shirt. What I mean is that I believe God asks each of us to define who we are, get to know our *selves*, and then to listen for Spirit's clear, soft voice whispering guidance in our ear. I loved my mother very much, and there were many positive ways she influenced my life, but I cannot hear what God is telling me if I am still listening to my mother.

Years before this new awareness, one of my favorite rituals was watching my mother transform herself from a rather plain daytime matron into a socialite stepping out into the sophisticated and glittering nighttime world of Manhattan. These were intimate moments with my mother and I cherished them. I knew she loved and cared about me, but she often seemed like she was millions of miles away. I could feel, and actually see, her leave the room and the present moment. It would begin with her eyes. Her attention shifted, and she was no longer focused on me or what I was saying. I don't know where she went, but I do know she had "gone" into her very own world, a place where no one could follow, and at times I felt shut out and abandoned.

But these moments of getting ready to go out were different. At eight or nine I felt good when she paid attention to what I had to say and relied on my advice on what to wear and what to do about her hair. I guess I wouldn't be lying when I say my mother was always upset about her hair.

I'd lie on my stomach with my body spread across my mother's twin bed pushed up close to my father's twin bed, watching her. Mummy stood in front of her dressing table mirror looking at her reflection with a scowl.

"It's just so thin," she moaned, teasing her hair in a frenzy. "I can't do anything with it."

"Try more spray," I'd advise.

She gave a big sigh and picked up the can of Revlon, spraying a thick layer of chemicals that settled like glue on her hair. The amount of spray she used would have kept her hairdo in place if there was a hurricane blowing through New York. It also created the illusion of thicker hair. (She went to the beauty parlor just once a week for a shampoo and set, and like so many women in the 1950's, slept with curlers and a pink curler cap every night.)

My mother's head was not the only place the hairspray accumulated. I noticed that the spray that missed her hair had clouded her mirror and distorted her image, like the mirror in the fun house. Once teased and combed into place, Mummy's thin brown hair fell gracefully into a page boy. She parted her hair on the side and pinned it back and off her face. Instead of the usual daytime gold barrette, she wore a diamond one on formal occasions. She didn't have bangs like I did.

"Just us two girls, sweetie," Mummy said as she put her brush down and picked up her lipstick. She turned and smiled one of her warmest smiles at me. I sat up then and watched closely as she carefully applied her makeup. She used a damp sponge to swab Max Factor pancake powder on her face, painted her full lips bright red, and grimaced slightly as she used just a little brown mascara and eyeliner on her upper lashes and lower lids. Then she picked up the bottle of her favorite Shalimar perfume and made small circular motions around her head, spraying herself with the French scent that did not mix well with "eau de Revlon."

"Oh, what should I wear?" she asked me, sipping her scotch, affectionately known as her "dressing drink."

"The black silk with the green sash, then you can wear the pearl and jade bracelet and you'll match," I offered, so proud that she wanted my opinion. "And the shoes," I added, "wear the green silk shoes with the rhinestone clips."

"Oh no, dearie, that would be too much. We'd never want to appear to do anything to excess, it just isn't done."

"Why not, Mummy?"

"Because it is important not to call attention to yourself," she replied.

"But I thought you get all pretty so people will look at you?" I was confused. Mummy came over and sat down beside me on the bed. Now I had her full attention.

"Well," she began, "your grandmother told me, and now I will tell you. It is important to be understated even if you have money. If you are flamboyant then it will look like you come from 'new money.'"

"What's 'new money?'" I asked.

"Oh," she sighed, "it's hard to explain. It is when people have a lot of money but take it for granted and spend it frivolously. We call those people the *nouveau riche*, she added.

Anyone who knew my mother would agree that Betty was an incurable romantic; and, from a very young age, I was influenced by the importance my mother placed on romance. She loved romantic movies and all those dreamy men like Cary Grant and Gregory Peck. She would laugh when I told her I thought she was as beautiful as Grace Kelly, and her reply was always, "Oh sweetie, never in a million years will I be as beautiful as Grace Kelly."

Mummy loved to dance to her favorite songs of the 1930's and 40's. I remember her two-stepping around the kitchen in her red and white checked apron, holding a wooden spoon she was using to stir the white sauce. Her eyes were closed and she had that far-off look on her face as Ella Fitzgerald crooned "Let's Fall in Love" from the hi fi in the living room. In moments like these, she could let herself go and be lost in an idealistic, romantic world. I think the love songs and movies of that time gave her hope. They helped her, and many other women, dance themselves into the illusion that their lives would end happily ever after.

My mother's happily-ever-after world came crashing down when my father left. Up until the moment he actually shut the door behind him she believed he wouldn't leave her. Two years earlier, after I found the Easter card, they took a trip to Europe with the hope of salvaging the marriage. When they arrived home Mummy's eyes were sparkling, and I knew that the trip had been a success.

"Oh Lisa," she told me, for now at twelve I had become her confidant, "it was so romantic in Italy. Daddy and I are in love again." Two years later he asked her for a divorce.

When I look back on this time in our lives, I realize how inappropriate it was for my mother to usher me into the personal details of her marriage as if I was a friend. I also understand that the level of her denial was destructive and naïve. I have seen that, in certain ways, she pushed my father away. I have been angry with her for not being "the perfect mother." Now that I am in my early sixties, twelve years older than she was when she died, I have reached a place of deep compassion and forgiveness. My heart has opened to this woman who was my mother, and I can witness her life without the needs of the child foremost in my mind.

Her message to me on having a successful, happily-ever-after life was, "Dearie, always remember how important it is to rise above things," and for a long time I took that to mean rise above your *feelings*, don't look at what is really in front of you, stay in the romantic movie. In essence, don't feel. But of course she felt, and the eczema all over her body showed me just how much stress she was under. At forty-four when her breast cancer came back, she was told she had six months to live. She survived another six *years*. I believe now that her message "to rise above" was really one of hope, that she knew how very important it was to be positive, to not dwell on the negative. I am sure it was her attitude that things *will* get better that kept her alive long enough to hold her first two grandchildren in her arms and to remarry and move to Connecticut. She spent her last few years there with a man who adored her and fulfilled a life-long dream of living in the country. She never gave up the belief that she could live on the "sunny side of the street."

My mother may have been in denial, but she never became bitter or resentful. She didn't let her difficulties obscure her charm. She had the kind of charm a person cannot acquire but is born with. In her high school year book her "saving grace" was warmth, and her best feature was her eyes. She had warm, doe-like brown eyes, the kind of eyes that drew people in, especially my teenage friends. They told me, "You are so lucky to have a mother like yours," and "I wish my mother was as easy to talk to as your mother is," and I agreed. When she knew I was having troubles with a boyfriend she would leave loving notes on my pillow. When she began dating my stepfather, he was like a teenager herself. Her romantic nature had her dancing to Gershwin again. They both knew her cancer could come back and that she probably didn't have many years left. Rather than turn her back on hope and be afraid of the future, she decided to live in the moment. She had a choice, and she chose to be happy with whatever time she had left.

Now, when I close my eyes and remember her dancing and singing along to Ella, with that dreamy look in her eyes, I see myself dancing beside her, full of the same romantic spirit. As a woman, I understand that it isn't wise to be too attached to romance. It can keep you living in an idealistic, illusionary world. Of course it doesn't change reality, but it can give life more sweetness and color. Being romantic reminds me of days gone by, and I am sure its presence in the culture served to help women of my mother's generation get through a depression and a world war. I wonder if my children's generation will know the hopeful, lovely feelings that romance can add to difficult times.

I always thought there would be time to say goodbye. I had seen her just ten days earlier, and she was very ill but still up and around. No one, not even her doctor, expected her to pass away suddenly in her sleep. My daughters and I were on our way to the circus in Boston when we got the call. They were seven and four, and the three of us sobbed in each other's arms for this woman we all loved so much.

The dogwood trees my mother loved were in full bloom the day she was buried. It was May 1972, and she had lived with cancer for the last fifteen of her fifty years in this lifetime. When Lee and I went to the funeral home to say goodbye to her body, I knew she would have been happy about the way she looked. She had asked to be buried in the beige and cream chiffon dress that she had worn to her wedding four years earlier. I was glad she had decided to forgo the Jackie O pillbox hat. What struck me as especially wonderful was that in death she had a long neck, and I remembered her often saying, "Oh that Audrey Hepburn, to have a long neck like hers."

Mummy was so completely still. I kept waiting for her to breathe a little, take a sigh; any tiny bit of movement would have been comforting. If I could only feel her squeeze my hand or see her eyes flutter open, just for a second. I wanted another moment with her alive; then she could leave.

A HAPPIER ENDING

LIKE THE RIVER THAT I grew up by in Manhattan, and the tidal river in Maine I looked out on for seven years after I moved there, my journey has led me into currents of thought and action that have kept me moving, both spiritually and physically. Life is showing me that the things I thought I wanted, and that I thought could make me happy, are temporary and cannot be held onto for very long. If I truly want to be happy then I need to learn to let go, to be in the river and float with the current, trusting that the flow and movement of God will take me to where I need to be. I imagine myself joining the river. I don't want to stand on the bank as an observer. I want to be part of the flow.

When my parents divorced and death took them away I had to dive into uncharted waters before I knew how to swim. I felt like I was drowning, and I tried to keep my head above water, gulping for air. As a child, I didn't understand that all our experiences in life, good or bad, are part of the flow. Now that I am a more conscious adult, I have learned that in order to go deeper into self I must be willing to let the river's current take me to the unknown places around the bend. When there are turbulent rapids to navigate and I am afraid, God's grace keeps guiding me back to smoother water.

Like the movement of a tidal river, where the river runs into the sea, I believe that one's life experiences mingle and change configuration. I am trying to be, like the tidal river, in the continuum of the flow. I do not think of life as a river that flows in only one direction, from the mountain to the sea. Instead, I think our lives are lived as a constant in and out motion, like making love, the motion of creation. There is no beginning or end to the ebb and flow of the journey, and it is always bringing us into new life.

There have been so many times since my parents' deaths when I have wished, with all my heart, that I could have changed the flow of their lives and that my brother and I had been able to watch them grow old together. I have felt the despair of knowing I couldn't save them no matter how hard I tried, or how hard I prayed. Recently, however, through my work with a therapy that allows for the possibility of creating a new life script, my imagination has rewritten the end of my parents' story. I have created a happy ending for them. Who is to say that in some parallel universe this new story isn't going on?

We are standing together on the shore of a river and I am handing my parents this book. I have wrapped it in a colorful, old blanket, the one that lies at the end of my bed in my childhood home in Maine. My father takes the book, bowing slightly to me. He is older, more distinguished, yet his face has remained virtually unlined. I notice that his black patch is gone and his hazel eyes are clear. He looks happy, content. As I watch him in this new story, he unwraps the book and turns toward my mother so they can look through the pages. They seem very pleased, and I know they will read it and take good care of this story.

After a few moments, Mummy carefully covers it again, and turning to me with one of her warmest smiles says, "Sweetie, we are so very proud of you." Daddy nods in agreement and the three of us hug goodbye.

Then my parents get into a canoe, and once they are settled, I shove them off from the river bank. I watch them as they begin their paddle downstream. Mummy is sitting in the stern, dressed in a faded blue fleece jacket and a crocheted green and blue cap that covers most of her hair, which has a few streaks of grey but is still nearly all brown. What I notice particularly is that they look healthy and robust, untouched by the suffering that kept them from living longer and more positive lives. They are together, and they seem happy and excited to be taking this new adventure on the river. Most important, though, is that I realize I am no longer responsible for their lives.

The river's current is moving fast, so the canoe is carried away quickly. Just before they float around the bend, Betty and Bev turn around and wave to me. Then they disappear from my sight. I stand on the bank awhile, feeling joy and gratitude for them. Then I slip into the river. Any feelings of anger or resentment that I have had in the past are washed away. I am choosing to be in the current of the blessing.

TRUST FUND BABY

I REMEMBER WHEN I WAS twelve and my seventh grade report card lay open on my father's desk in the living room. Daddy had just gotten home from work, had made a cocktail, and before he sat down he walked over to the desk, picked up the card, then sank into his easy chair, ready to talk. Mummy was sitting on the couch, and I sat next to her.

"Not as many A's and B's this semester, Lisa," Daddy began, frowning slightly. "You've even managed to get a few C's; what happened?"

"I don't know, Daddy," I replied nervously, waiting for a big lecture.

"Now Bev," Mummy chimed in, "don't be too hard on her. It's not as if she's going to have to worry about college or find a job afterwards." Then turning to me with a patronizing smile, she said, "Besides, sweetie, girls get married and raise a family. But it is good to always try and do your best," she added as an afterthought.

From a very young age I was assured that because I had been "blessed" with a trust fund from my grandfather, I would always be financially secure. Although the principle could never be spent, the income would most certainly be enough to meet my needs. People in our social class brought up their children to assume that the money they did have would always be there. Either you had a trust fund or you would marry a man or woman who did. Because of this legacy, we were promised protection from an "ordinary" life, and some of us grew up believing that we really were "blessed." We were "Trust Fund Babies" after all.

There was a certain amount of social prestige and money surrounding my family. I went to school with the Rockefellers and to dancing school with the son of New York's mayor. But Mummy would always remind me that we were really not considered that wealthy compared to other upper-class WASP families in Manhattan. Then, as if to illustrate her point, she would sigh, with that faraway look in her eyes, and tell me a family story:

"Your great-grandfather Barstow was a good friend of old John D. Rockefeller and became a director of Standard Oil. When John D. asked Frank to invest $1,000 in his new company Frank told him no, he didn't have the money. Just think how different things would be if he had," she said with another big sigh.

Trust funds are like parents. They take care of you, and they continue to after your parents die. They are not flesh and bone, however. They are invisible bodies that live in banks and are tended by men in three-piece navy blue suits. Their mode of communication is bank slips that are mailed each month saying: "X amount of dollars has been transferred from the trust department into your checking account."

When my step-grandfather died in 1952, I was named as a recipient of a third-generation trust and without knowing it, began to be groomed to join the small, elite group of the financially independent. In spite of my mother's warnings not to take this gift for granted, I did begin to develop a rather *laissez-faire* attitude about it. The messages I received about having money were essentially that I was different and quite separate from the rest of the world. As if to impose this sense of separation even further, Papa left his money in trust to "female issue" only. It was his belief that men should work for their money and women should not. "It's not as if you'll have to work, sweetie," my mother's proclamation kept repeating itself for so long in my mind that I truly believed it. In the 1950's, the idea that work for females was something that could build confidence and self-esteem, and be interesting and motivational, was for the most part unexplored. By the time I began to wonder if I had missed an opportunity to grow through a career, I was too entrenched in a lifestyle of "freedom" to imagine taking a nine-to-five job. The work I did do as an adult was always on my own terms, and I never made enough money to support myself. I didn't have to.

When I was eight Daddy took me downtown to Wall Street to the bank where my trust fund was. We walked into the enormous lobby with a ceiling as high as the Metropolitan Museum of Art. I looked at the historic scenes of New York created by tiny pieces of colored mosaic tiles.

"Oh Daddy," I exclaimed, impressed by this huge hall, "is this really where my trust fund lives?"

Then, as if to answer me, Daddy took me over to a lady who sat behind a brass cage and said, "Excuse me Ma'am, I'd like my daughter to see a one-thousand dollar bill. Do you have one that you could show her?" The lady smiled at me, then opened a drawer and brought one out. She slipped it through the opening under the cage, keeping her hand on it while I looked at it for a long time. I had never seen bills larger than the twenties Mummy and Daddy had in their wallet.

We left the bank and walked a few blocks over to the New York Stock Exchange Building. As we stood outside looking up at its impressive granite façade, Daddy said, "See this building, Lisa? This is where your trust fund *really* lives."

Over the years, I have found that because of prejudice or envy, my financial independence has created distance and separation. Before I began to wake up and expand "out of the box," I often protected myself by being aloof, and found that my sense of entitlement had disengaged me from people whose lives were different from mine. I wasn't entirely taken in by money or a privileged lifestyle, however, and as an adult I began to understand how many experiences in life money cannot protect a person from. I have seen how it can stifle consciousness and spiritual growth if it is taken for granted or seen as an omnipresent source of happiness. One of the most important things I have learned about being the recipient of a trust fund is to let go of guilt. This was a gift I was given, and I shall always be grateful for it.

MARY MCMANUS

OVER THE YEARS LEE AND I had several different govern-
esses, and our favorite one was Mary McManus, who came to
live with us when my brother was three and I was seven. Mary
was a small, robust, jovial Scottish woman from Glasgow, who
seemed too full of fun to be called something as formal as a
governess. Her wiry, prematurely grey hair was cut short, and I
was sure she never wore hairspray or curlers at night like
Mummy. She had a marvelous Scottish brogue and a twinkle in
her eye. Mary always seemed happy, and it felt good to be
around her.

She slept in a tiny bedroom off the kitchen pantry that was
just big enough for a twin bed, a small dresser, and a corner
sink. A window faced the courtyard below. The bathroom
was cramped with a toilet and a bathtub that someone with
a sizeable girth wouldn't fit into. Lucky for Mary, she was
petite.

Mary loved tea. I remember her sitting at the Formica
kitchen table wedged between the window and the sink, drinking her special English tea in an enormous cup. She didn't use
Lipton tea bags like Mummy. Instead, she had her own tin can-
ister decorated with pink and lavender flowers, which she told
me were English primroses and posies. Her special tin con-

tained loose tea leaves, and when she was ready for a cup, which was almost always, she would put the leaves in a small silver ball with holes in it and submerge it into the cup of boiling water, letting it steep before adding milk and sugar. I loved to watch the steam from the tea curl its way up toward the kitchen ceiling. After the milk and sugar were added and she had gently blown the heat away, I'd ask her for a sip.

Mary was in charge of Lee and me. She got up with us in the morning while Mummy and Daddy slept, prepared our meals, washed our clothes, and took us to the park to play when we weren't in school. On rainy days she sat on the floor in my bedroom and played Parcheesi and Canasta with me, checkers with Lee.

"Mary, do you think you'll get married someday?" I asked her one afternoon while we were playing cards. I didn't know how old she was, but I had figured out that if she was thinking of tying the knot she had better hurry up.

"Oh no, my girlie, I am content just as I am."

At nine I wasn't too sure about that word "content." It sounded nice, and despite my young age, I understood that content wasn't something either of my parents felt very often, if ever. I would say that content was Mary singing a Scottish tune while she made a meal, humming softly as she ironed my dancing-school dresses, and sitting by herself at the kitchen table sipping her tea.

One summer when we went to Maine, Mary took a long vacation back home to Scotland. She was so excited to see her family. I was worried that she wouldn't come back in the fall, that I would never see her again. I wondered why she would want to come back. After all, her family was there, not in America with us.

"I hope you will come back to us, Mary," I told her one day as she was packing me up to go to Maine. I watched as she folded my shorts, tee shirts, and summer dresses, taking care to smooth them out before placing another article of clothing on top.

She stopped packing, and looking kindly at me, she answered, "Of course I will, wee one. I love Scotland, but New York and America are so big, so interesting. I think Scotland is too small for me now."

When Mary returned from Glasgow at the end of the summer, she brought Lee and me gifts. For Lee, she had picked out a tan Shetland sweater and blue-watch tartan wool shorts. She also bought him a doll dressed as one of the British Beefeaters, who, she explained, were the men who guard the crown jewels in the Tower of London.

"Oh, that doll looks just like the man on Daddy's bottle of gin," I exclaimed, proud of myself for pointing it out.

"What did you bring for me, Mary?" I asked her impatiently. I couldn't wait to open the large box sitting on the kitchen table.

"Here, open it," she replied, handing the gift and the scissors to me.

I quickly cut the twine that held the box together, took off the lid and removed the tissue. Inside the box was an authentic Scottish Highlands costume. There was a green plaid kilt, white cotton shirt with puffy sleeves, black wool vest with silver buttons, thick green wool knee socks, and a cap made from the same tartan as the kilt, with two black grosgrain ribbons that hung down the back. I was speechless.

"Try it on, see if it fits," she said, her grey-green eyes twinkling at me.

When I came out of her room, I was a Scot, just like her. The clothes fit me perfectly. All I needed were my black patent leather shoes, the ones I wore to dancing school.

"Now that you have the costume, I can teach you the Highland Fling," Mary said, getting out of her chair. "I know how much you love to dance."

So, there in the kitchen I had my first lesson in the dance of Mary's homeland. She showed me how to twirl my kilt, keep my arms up to form a circle over my head, how to kick my legs and feet and fling my body. After a few more lessons, I was "flinging" myself all over the apartment.

One night while they were preparing their cocktails in the pantry, Mummy and Daddy asked me to come into the living room and dance the Highland Fling for them. "Go put your costume on," Daddy said. "I'll go find the Scottish dance record I have."

Moments later, I proudly walked into the living room. Daddy was in his easy chair, Lee and Mummy were sitting on the couch, and Mary was standing at the door. I looked over at her as Daddy turned the record on, and she winked at me. Then I began to dance the dance of Scotland as the wee lassie I was, and in that moment, I wondered if this was what it felt like to be content.

A year later, Mary left us.

When Mummy had told me she was leaving I ran sobbing into Mary's room. "You and Lee are older now and do not need a nanny any longer," she said, holding me tight. "I have been trained to take care of babies, and I am going to a family with a new baby." I noticed that Mary had tears in her eyes when she added, "But I shall miss you both very, very much. You and Lee are very dear to me." Then she hugged me close and I clung tightly to her, knowing that Lee's and my life would not feel as happy without her.

"I will always remember you, Mary," I cried. She had lived with us for four years. Now she was going to leave us and go take care of other children.

Later that day I told Mummy how sad I was. "Oh I know, sweetie," she answered, "we will all miss her. But let's be happy for her that she will be able to take care of a new baby who needs her."

I didn't want to be happy for another child, but I knew Mummy would be disappointed if I wasn't, so I pretended and acted like it was all right. But I knew I would never forget her.

CHRISTMAS IN NEW YORK

CHRISTMAS WAS A MAGICAL TIME in New York. The season began with the Macy's Day Parade at Thanksgiving when Santa Claus was ushered down Broadway on a red and green float, stepping off at the front door of the department store where he was in residence for the weeks before Christmas. Daddy took Lee and me to the parade every year. He had a friend whose office looked down on Broadway so we could see it without freezing. I thought it would have been more fun to be down on the street with everyone else, though.

Mummy never came. She stayed home to cook the turkey and make dinner for Daddy's family. It had become a family tradition to have my grandmother Gommy and her children and grandchildren together at our apartment.

I loved my older cousins. Even though they were teenagers, they played with Lee and me and teased us good naturedly. They came all the way from Buffalo, and when I was eleven they moved to California, which, in the mid-fifties, seemed extremely exotic and a million miles away.

My grandmother always carved the turkey. She sat at the head of the table, in Daddy's seat, and sharpened the large carving knife with the bone handle that had been my grandfather's. "You need strong wrists to carve," she told us all and would proceed, with determined ease, to slice the waiting bird. Gommy always wore six charm bracelets on her right wrist, and when she carved, they jingled so loudly she could barely hear us answer if we wanted light or dark meat. I always asked for "lots of everything." Everyone laughed when I said that, but I didn't understand what was so funny. How could anyone not want lots of everything?

Gommy's real name was Theodora, or Dora, as everyone called her, and when she was young she was an accomplished equestrian and skippered her own boat during race week on Martha's Vineyard. She had thick, copper-penny hair and deep-set, sea-green eyes. Mummy told me that when Gommy was young, people considered her quite beautiful. But now she looked very old and wrinkled, and I was fascinated by the fact that she appeared to have no bosoms. Her chest was totally flat, like mine.

My best memory of Gommy is when she was in her mid-eighties and I would go visit her at tea time.

"Won't you join me and have a cocktail?" she asked as the clock chimed four o'clock.

"Oh no thanks, Gommy, it's a little early for me." Then Nellie, a loyal and dear woman who had worked for my grandmother since she was sixteen and was now in her eighties as well, brought in a pot of tea for me and an old-fashioned glass filled with bourbon, and only one ice cube, for Gommy. As she swirled the bourbon around the ice for quite a while before taking her first sip, I noticed that her bracelets were still jangling loudly and her fingers were gnarled with arthritis.

"How have you been feeling, Gommy?" I asked her, observing that she was quite pale and the circles under her eyes were dark and deep. Her auburn hair had turned grey long ago, but it was dyed brown and was still brown when she died a few years later, at eighty-seven.

"Well, dear," she replied, "I haven't been feeling too well, and the other day I realized that I have to limit my activities."

"What activities do you mean, Gommy?"

"I go to church every Sunday and get my hair done at the Westbury every Wednesday. I can't do both anymore, so I'm going to give up church."

After Thanksgiving, Manhattan dressed itself up for Christmas, and FAO Schwarz wasn't the only store that displayed festive windows. One year, Tiffany's had miniature trees decorated with ruby and emerald rings, diamonds sparkling at the top like stars. Saks Fifth Avenue had a choir of angels standing over the entrance singing carols piped over a loudspeaker, and across the street, on the promenade at Rockefeller Center, another host of angels dressed in white and gold blew golden trumpets, leading us down to the enormous tree.

"Look at that beautiful tree, children," Mummy said as we hung over the wall watching the skaters going round and round beneath the giant evergreen. "You know it comes from the woods of northern Maine," she added proudly.

The sweet aroma of roasting chestnuts filled the air, and we'd stop at one of the carts that had an oven with a chimney where the smoke came out. A man who was dressed in shabby clothes and looked very cold stood beside the cart. He had small paper bags set out, filled with the roasted nuts, and since Lee and I didn't like chestnuts, Mummy would buy a bag to bring home to Daddy.

Outside most stores on Fifth Avenue, Santa's helpers rang bells and cried "Merry Christmas," and Mummy always had some change to give us to put in the red metal bucket that looked like a wishing well.

If we were really lucky, snow would fall and cover the city, transforming the hard grey and black asphalt to a landscape of soft white. When snow falls in Manhattan, the entire city seems embraced by the hush of its gentle movement falling out of the sky. There is a dream-like silence—no more car horns or screaming ambulance sirens, only the wispy quiet sound of snow coming down.

"Christmas is the time of year when I am glad we live in New York," Mummy told us as we walked up the Avenue. It was good to hear her say this because the rest of the year she would sigh and say how much she wished she lived in the country, which for most of my childhood was my wish too.

The holiday season began for me with the ceremony of the lighting of the Park Avenue Christmas trees, performed every year outside our church that was situated at the top of Park Avenue, on 91st Street. You had a perfect view down the Avenue to the Grand Central Building at the bottom. Everyone sang carols, and there was a special concert by the junior choir. When it was just getting dark, Dr. Wolfe, the minister, flipped the switch, and every tree for forty-five blocks came alive with shining white lights and golden stars at the top. Then the cross appeared. In the center of the darkened Grand Central Building, just enough office lights had been left on to form an enormous cross that looked like it was suspended in the air. That was my favorite part of the ceremony.

"Well, I guess we're in the Christmas spirit now," Daddy laughed; then he whistled through his fingers for a cab to take us home. After we were settled in the taxi, he told the driver, "Make sure you take us down Park to 57th Street. We want to see all these beautiful lights." Lee and I sat on the jump seats just in front of Mummy and Daddy, who sat close together, and our family watched happily as our Christmas city went speeding by.

My parents took the traditions of both their families seriously. A German one, passed down from my maternal great-grandmother, was that Santa Claus decorated the tree. A few days before Christmas, Mummy and I went down to our storage unit in the basement to find the tree stand and the boxes of decorations and lights. Daddy always took Christmas Eve Day off from work, and he, Lee, and I walked up to First Avenue in the morning where trees were sold outside the grocery stores in the neighborhood. Our tree was delivered in the afternoon, and Daddy moved the furniture around in the living room to make room for it.

Gommy arrived at five o'clock sharp, and after drinks were made for the grownups, hot chocolate and marshmallows for Lee and me, Daddy began the chore of putting the lights on the tree. Mummy was in charge of the tinsel. Every year they argued about whether to use the garland or the icicle kind. Mummy usually won, and they wrapped rope garlands around the tree.

After dinner Gommy read the *The Night Before Christmas*, and then Lee and I hung up our stockings and went to bed. Once Gommy had left, my parents decorated the tree, assembled the toys, stuffed our stockings, finished the wrapping, and positioned everything perfectly under the tree. Mummy always counted the presents to make sure Lee and I had an equal amount.

The living room had French doors that Daddy closed before they went to bed in the early hours of the morning, and when Lee and I woke up a few hours later, Daddy snuck into the living room to turn the tree lights on. As Mummy opened the doors, he was ready with his camera to get a picture of our amazement when we saw the magically decorated tree. Each year I thought it was the most beautiful sight I had ever seen. Besides the lights, ornaments, and tinsel, Mummy had sprayed the tree with fake snow, and it looked for a moment as though Santa Claus had brought the soft beauty of a snowfall into our living room.

Another tradition, and one that I hated, was that after we had had breakfast and opened all our presents my father would get up from our cozy family circle and go to a party at his men's club. He changed from his bathrobe and pajamas into a morning suit with tails ("Daddy looks like a penguin!" Lee would exclaim) and a top hat. The club hosted a gathering called a "Fish House Punch Party" on Christmas morning. Women and children were not invited.

Daddy's club was a source of constant discontent in our family. During the week, before coming home in the evening, Daddy often stopped for a game of squash and a cocktail or two at his club on Park Avenue. I remember Mummy waiting for him to come home. She sat in the living room with the evening paper and her scotch on the rocks with a splash, drawing deeply on a Tareyton cigarette. Sometimes if it got late and dinner was ready, she would call the club to ask if Daddy was still there. But the answer was always the same. "Oh, Mrs. Barstow," the man on the other end of the line would say, "you know that we are not allowed to divulge our members' whereabouts."

"Do you have to go again this year, Bev?" Mummy asked him every Christmas morning. "We are having such a nice family time. Please don't go." She looked so sad and tired.

"This is a tradition, Betty," Daddy told her. "I'm not going to miss it. It's important to me. I'll see you in a little while at your mother's for lunch."

Then he left Mummy, Lee, and me sitting in the midst of brightly colored Christmas paper and red and green ribbon. New toys were strewn about the living room, and Bing Crosby was singing "Have Yourself a Merry Little Christmas" on the hi fi. This was the moment for me when the magic of the season was over. Daddy had left and Mummy looked sad. Everything had changed.

On special occasions around the Christmas and Easter holidays, as promised, Nanny took me to the theater or Radio City Music Hall. When I went to the Music Hall I dreamed about being a Rockette for days afterwards. As the dancers formed a line across the stage, I was fascinated that they were all the exact same height and their legs, raised in the air, matched up perfectly.

I loved Broadway. During *Peter Pan,* I fell in love with the boy who never wanted to grow up, wishing with all my heart that I could be Wendy. In *South Pacific,* I was entranced by the beautiful love songs and the idea of living on an island way out in the Pacific Ocean.

After each performance, David, Nanny's chauffeur, picked us up and delivered us at the Plaza Hotel for high tea in the Palm Court. In the 1950's, the Palm Court was as gracious and glamorous as any café in Europe.

Nanny and I sat at a small table in the middle of the Court, separated from the hotel lobby by tall palms in enormous blue and white Chinese urns. The round tables, covered in pale pink damask cloths, were placed so close together that Nanny had to keep *shh*-ing me.

"You really don't want the people sitting next to us joining in our conversation," she told me quietly. When Nanny was annoyed her eyes got smaller and she pursed her lips tightly.

"OK, Nanny," I said in a whisper. "Oh, but isn't it beautiful here?" I added enthusiastically.

Miniature golden lamps lit each table, and all around the perimeter of the Court there were large gold filigree pedestals with arms like branches on a tree. They were holding big white balls lighted from within and glowing like candlelight. As the room filled up with the sounds of tea-time chatter, a man dressed in a tuxedo strolled by our table playing German waltzes on his violin. Soon the room was full of romantic music as well.

I loved having tea with my grandmother in the Palm Court. I had gotten all dressed up and was wearing my new deep purple wool coat with the velvet collar that Mummy had ordered from London. Nanny wore her black wool coat and had a dead fox wrapped around her shoulders. Its little marble eyes stared at me, and I was fascinated by the way its mouth clipped onto its tail. There were lots of ladies wearing furs at the Palm Court.

As we listened to the music, I leaned over the table and said in my lowest voice possible, "I absolutely loved *South Pacific*, Nanny, especially the part when Mary Martin washed her hair on the stage and got the people in the front row all wet!" Nanny laughed, agreeing that the musical had been delightful.

"Let's order some tea before it gets too late," she said, signaling a waiter. I watched as he began to push a pastry cart toward us. It was filled with *éclairs*, cream puffs, fruit tarts, and Napoleons. When he arrived at our table and asked me which pastry I would like and how I took my tea, I replied:

"One of each please, and lots of cream and sugar."

"Certainly you don't mean you want every pastry on the tray, Miss," the waiter said, looking alarmed.

Well of course I wanted every one, but I knew that it wouldn't be polite, so I laughed and said in my most grown-up voice, "Oh no, I was only teasing. I'll take those three," pointing to the *éclair,* the Napoleon, and the cream puff that came with chocolate sauce, too.

After we finished and Nanny paid the bill, we crossed the hotel lobby and went outside. David had been waiting in the long line of limousines in front of the hotel, and when he saw us, he pulled right up to the steps and hopped out of the car to open the back door for us. Dusk had begun to settle over the city, and tiny white lights twinkled everywhere in the plaza. It looked like stars had been sprinkled on all the small evergreen trees that stood beside the splashing fountain across from the hotel.

On our way home, David drove past FAO Schwarz, my favorite toy store. Its Christmas windows were on display and they looked like the inside of Geppetto's toy store. Hidden behind painted wooden cutouts were motors that brought the shop to life. They moved all the marionettes that looked like elves dancing and cutting wood. Geppetto was carving his special boy.

"Oh, look at that," I cried. "I wish we could stop and really see."

"Not now, Lisa," Nanny said. "It's late, and your mother will wonder where we are. We'll come back another day."

I leaned back in the comfortable seat and played with the button that made the window go up and down between the front, where David sat, and the back, where Nanny and I were sitting. When I was alone with David, I sat up front with him, but now I snuggled close to my grandmother. A light rain was beginning to fall, and the drops reflected the city lights on the windshield, leaving splashes of red and green that moved back and forth through the wipers. I was entranced. It looked as though the traffic lights were bringing Christmas right into the car.

By the time David turned onto Sutton Place, I had fallen fast asleep.

IMPERMANENCE

AS I SIT DOWN BESIDE my grandmother, I notice how small and unfamiliar she looks in the big hospital bed. I don't like the way her mouth droops on one side and that she can't talk to me. Her eyes are closed, but when she hears me move the chair closer to the bed, she opens her left eye into a narrow slit and peers at me. At sixty-one, Nanny has suffered a stroke. I am frightened, and I am sure she is frightened too.

Mummy has brought a pretty, pale blue blanket cover and a lace bed jacket from home. A manicurist just left, and Nanny's hands, with their perfectly shaped and polished nails, are resting on top of the cover. Their blood-red color contrasts with the bright white hospital sheet.

"You have such beautiful nails, Nanny," I tell her as I lift her right hand and place it gently in mine. Our eyes meet again, and although she can't answer me, I know she understands. Her short brown hair is tangled and matted in the back. It reminds me of the sparrow's nest I saw in the park the other day.

"Would you like me to brush your hair?" I ask her. With some effort, she slowly nods, and I take the hairbrush lying on the table next to the bed, carefully lifting her head off the pillow, and begin to softly brush her tangled hair. When I am finished, I sit beside my grandmother, crying quietly, until Mummy arrives and takes me home.

My heart broke when Nanny died. She passed away at home after receiving twenty-four-hour nursing care for many months. I had never seen a dead person before. How could anyone be so completely still? The day she died, the minister from our church arrived, and our family gathered around her bed to say some prayers. Mummy was crying softly as Rev. Wolf recited the Twenty-Third Psalm, and Daddy put his arm around her. He looked sad also. I wondered if he was upset because he yelled at Mummy about Nanny being in our living room so many times when he came home from work. I also wondered about the sadness that seemed to cling to my grandmother, and all the fears that pressed against her life. I remembered Mummy once telling me that when she got older, she hoped she would be more like her grandmother than her mother. When I asked her why she replied, "Your great-grandmother was a happy woman, your Nanny is not. I want to be a happy person."

At twelve, I had never been to a funeral before, and I wasn't in the least bit prepared. I was in the chapel standing in the pew next to Papa's son, Uncle Willard, and we were singing "Oh God Our Help in Ages Past." My brother Lee was standing next to me and began fidgeting. "Stop it," I hissed. "Be still." I looked at the pew in front of me and noticed that Mummy was crying again. Daddy gave her his handkerchief and squeezed her hand. Her brothers, Jimmy and Jack, were standing on her other side, and they looked very sad but weren't crying. As we began to sing the second verse the doors to the outside swung open and the pallbearers rolled Nanny's casket down the aisle.

It was covered in a blanket of baby's breath and white lilies, and the early spring sun flooded the sanctuary with light. I was overwhelmed and felt something heavy push itself into the middle of my body. I let out a loud sob, and without any warning I began to shake. A chest full of sobs that I could no longer contain filled the chapel like the light. I was out of control. A moment later, my step-uncle put his hand on my shoulder and led me out of the chapel. Once I had calmed down I felt embarrassed. No one else had been making so much noise.

Nothing was the same in our family after Nanny died. It was as if the threads that connected all of us to the traditions of her generation started to unravel. Without her matriarchal presence as the container, the illusions that had held us all together broke into fragments that could not be put back together in just the same way. Like a Tibetan sand painting, the picture of my life, so finely crafted, began to blow away and disappear.

My illusions about God as the One who would fix things were shattered, and I stopped trusting in Him.

Before I grew into a woman's form, there were nights when I felt myself leave my body and travel far away. When my body "called" me back, I stripped my nightgown off, got out of bed, and lay naked on the hard wooden floor. I made sure the window was open so that the frigid winter air filled the room and it became uncomfortably cold. Lying in the dark, I tried to imagine what it would be like to sleep without warmth and shelter.

After a while, when I felt the cold in my bones, I moved my body back into my bed. Before the ritual began, I had stripped the bed of the top sheet, blanket, and quilt. I lay naked on the bed, still feeling some discomfort. Then I began to add comfort, a layer at a time. First I put my nightgown back on. Then I pulled the sheet and blanket, one at a time, over my body and placed the pillow under my head. Finally, I snuggled cozily under the pink sateen quilt. Feeling warm and safe I would fall asleep.

Perhaps this ritual was my attempt to provide a boundary for my body so that it would feel safe. If God wasn't answering my prayers, I had to replace this unseen deity with a tactile sense of definition and form. Was I afraid that if I didn't feel my body I would become invisible and disappear, like God? Obviously, I hadn't been good enough. God had deserted me, and my love and faith in Him had become conditional. I felt empty. Instead of God, food became my comfort so that I could feel my body and touch something real.

But I always kept wandering back to God hopeful that He would remember me. I waited, I prayed the self-centered prayers of a child, and I waited some more. Nothing got better. Cancer, alcoholism, divorce, and eventual death tied up in a big knot I had no idea how to unravel. I thought that was God's job. I didn't understand that when I was traveling over the door sill between the wilderness and a shaky faith, I was living in the place where the two worlds touch, asking for what I really wanted.

FIFTEEN TO EIGHTEEN

WHEN IT CAME TIME TO decide if I wanted to go away to boarding school or stay through twelfth grade at my school in New York, I chose to go away. My trust fund had been paying for my private school education, and I knew I was lucky to be given the choice.

The all-girls' school where I spent the first three years of the sixties is in a lovely rural part of Connecticut. It is situated on a picturesque New England green with a white Congregational Church on one side and 18th-century saltbox houses across from it. All 160 girls slept, ate, prayed, laughed, and studied together. We were housed in a large yellow stucco building that had been designed to look like a convent with a quadrangle in the middle. Although there was an increasing emphasis on providing a fine education, it wouldn't be out of place to say that, at the time, this was considered a "finishing school" for upper-class, privileged young ladies. I was very happy there and felt secure in the cloistered world. For the first time in three years, I didn't have to be in the middle of the tensions at home or keep an eye on my parents. Not being one to easily let go of thinking I had some control, however, I spent a good deal of time in the chapel and in the dining room across the hall, alternately praying and eating over the condition of my parents' marriage.

The summer before I left for boarding school, Mummy had a professional photographer in Maine come to our house and take a picture of her, Daddy, and Lee.

"I'll get a nice frame, and you can put it on your bureau at school. Then you can see us every day," she told me. In the picture, Mummy is wearing her favorite pale pink linen sheath, beige pumps, panty hose, and a strand of pearls. Both Daddy and my eleven-year-old brother are dressed in a coat and tie. The three of them are sitting stiffly on the deck of the Casino, with the bay in the background. They look disconnected from each other, not like a family at all. When I gazed at the photograph each morning I realized that rather than making me happy, it made me feel sad; I wondered, if this was a family photograph, why wasn't I in it as well? When my parents divorced a year later, I put the picture in the bottom drawer of my bureau. I understood then that this had been my mother's final attempt to create the illusion of a family intact.

My school had lots of rules. Although it was not Catholic, our worship time was taken very seriously. We went to chapel twice a day, and church on Sunday was mandatory. We were not allowed to leave the school alone, even for a walk, or to have boys come visit on Saturdays. Until I was a senior, I could take just one weekend home all year. Unlike many of my friends, I felt extremely comfortable with the structure. The rules provided me with boundaries, and living away from home helped me begin to give my personal life some definition.

I was fully engaged in sports, glee club, drama, making friends, and eating. Always on the alert for extra cinnamon buns at recess lunch and second helpings at meals, I also made sure I had an ample supply of candy in my room. I had access to the candy closet because I was a class officer, and every week-end I could get the key and take as much candy as I could stuff down the front of my uniform. One would think that with all this eating I was getting fat. My weight fluctuated somewhat, but after puberty I was finally feeling all right about the way I looked. I still would have liked to be as skinny as some of my friends, and I hated it when my roommate nicknamed me Steinway because of my un-tapered legs. But I felt very happy when I went home for vacation, and Mummy would concede that I had quite a nice figure.

Now and then I woke up enough to depart from the narrow-mindedness of adolescence and the constricted world of privilege. During sophomore year, I attended a religious conference at a nearby school and heard the Rev. William Sloan Coffin, who was the Chaplain of Yale Divinity School, speak about the civil rights movement in the South. I had never heard someone speak with so much passion before. He had witnessed the violence during marches and what the police did to the blacks when they stood up to injustice. His speech lifted me out of apathy just long enough to go back to school and demand to know why there weren't any Negro girls at our school.

"We did enroll one or two in the early fifties," the headmistress told me," but since then we haven't had any applications. It's probably a question of money." I thought about the conference for a while and read about the marches in the newspaper, but I was quickly distracted from any ideas I might have had about activism and chose, instead, "to go back to sleep."

My friends considered me lucky to have grown up in the sophisticated life of Manhattan. When I went home for Christmas and spring vacations I got dressed up in silk and velvet evening gowns and attended subscription dances with boys I had met at dancing school years before. My friends from Maine would come to visit and we went to nightclubs like Birdland to hear Count Basie, and the African Room, which ironically had become a popular hangout for preppies. The drinking age in New York was eighteen, and by the time I was sixteen I could get served. I was introduced to tropical drinks with umbrellas there and realized that my sugar cravings were easily satisfied by syrupy rum drinks of any kind. It was safe to drink in New York. No one had to drive anywhere. All you had to do was call a cab. When you arrived home, if you had difficulty maneuvering yourself through the front door of your building, the doorman was always there to help you.

One early spring weekend of my senior year, I was preparing to go back to school after visiting with Mummy and relaxing with my friend Robin, who had come down to the city with me. There were just a few months left before graduation and the beginning of the debutante season:

"Robin and I are leaving for Grand Central, Mummy," I yell from the hall. I pick my Polo coat up off the chair and put it on.

"Don't forget a hat, sweetie," Mummy reminds me as she walks into the front hall. "It's cold out today, and it's always colder in the country," she adds with questionable wisdom. She gives Robin a friendly kiss on the cheek, hugs and kisses me, then says, "I can't wait until your graduation when you and Lee will both be home. It gets a little lonely here without you."

Mummy is standing next to the front door while Robin and I wait for the elevator to come. She looks sad. Her hair is disheveled and matted in the back. It gets that way when she spends a lot of time on her chaise lounge, reading *Vogue* or taking a catnap. "Do you have enough money for a cab and the train?" she asks me as we are stepping onto the elevator. "Yes thanks, we're all set. I'll call you when I get there. Lots of love." Rarely does anyone in our family say "I love you."

The cab ride doesn't take long, and we reach the station with more than an hour to spare. "Robin, let's go to the Rough Rider Room and get a drink," I suggest.

"Great idea, you lead the way." Robin lives on Philadelphia's Mainline, where Mummy is originally from, and she isn't nearly as familiar with Manhattan as I am. But then, every preppie who travels from New York to go back to a New England boarding school is familiar with this particular bar in the Roosevelt Hotel. It has become a popular meeting place to end a weekend of freedom before returning to school.

Robin and I walk into the bar and immediately see a few other girls we know. "Come sit with us," Jody calls out when she sees us. She pushes over to make room for us on the red velvet banquette, moving her drink and ashtray over as well. When the waitress arrives Robin and I order whiskey sours.

"I'd like a few extra cherries in mine please," I tell her as she turns to go.

We talk about our weekend and order several more drinks. I love the way I feel after a few drinks, especially the sweet ones. I am what I imagine as "loose around the edges." I feel like I am letting go of control and am in more control all at the same time. I am funnier, smarter, and I feel more complete.

After we pay for our drinks and go into the station to buy our tickets for the train trip I am appalled when I realize that I am almost out of cash. I have spent most of my money on drinks. "Oh my God, I can't buy a ticket, does anyone have money they can lend me?"

"We only have enough for our tickets," they all chime in, giggling at the look on my face that is a cross between a teen-

ager who is three sheets to the wind on whiskey sours, and a
little kid who has gotten caught doing something bad.

"Oh shit," I moan, "what will I do?"

"Call your Mom," Robin suggests, "She can bring you
money. We have enough time."

"Yeah right: Hi Mom, I've just spent my train fare on drinks,
can you take a taxi to Grand Central please, and bail me out?
That would go over really well." Just then I spy a large sign
advertising Traveler's Aid. *Need help with traveling expenses?* "I'll be
right back," I yell to my friends over my shoulder, and I run up
the stairs of the terminal to find the office. Once inside, I sit
down and smile my friendliest smile at the nice lady who is going to give me my train fare back to school. She listens as I explain the situation and is kind enough not to ask what happened to my ticket money. She does ask where I live, however,
and when she hears Sutton Place, which is just twenty blocks
north of the station, her eyes narrow and she frowns at me. I
can tell she doesn't like me, especially now that she knows
where I live. I have begun to notice that when I tell people I
live on Sutton Place, their attitude toward me seems to change.

"We don't give money to kids who live in the same city,
whose parents are rich and can help them out. Just go home and
get your aid," she says, mocking me.

"But I'll miss the train. I won't get back to school on time,"
I mumble into my hand, trying to stop any whiskey sour fumes
from drifting in her direction.

"Then you'll be late. Too bad," she adds sarcastically. Then
she stands up and opens the door. I leave the office and find my
friends.

"We've got to go," they say. "What are you going to do?"

"I'm going home. I'll have to come up in the morning." I
feel like such a fool. How could I have been so stupid? When I

arrive in front of the building, John the doorman is there to open the cab door.

"I thought you were going back to school," he says when he sees me.

"I was," I reply meekly. "John, could you please ring my mother up on the house phone and ask her to come down to the lobby with her pocketbook? I need her to pay my cab fare." Mummy is furious when I tell her what happened. "I can't believe you would do such a stupid thing, Lisa," she admonishes me. "How embarrassing that you would go to Traveler's Aid. We are not a family who needs to go to a place like that." Even though she is angry, I am relieved. She doesn't seem nearly as concerned about the whiskey sours as she is about my asking for money.

Thankfully, during my senior year I began to awaken and expand beyond my limited lifestyle of drinking up my train fare, shopping, and going to dances and bars. I made a few friends at school who had different interests than I did. I was introduced to classical music. Some friends actually preferred it to rock and roll. I had never sat and listened to classical music before then, and I discovered that I loved Vivaldi. My friend Gay, who played the oboe and lived in a very intellectual New York household, told me that as classical composers go, Vivaldi created pleasant scores, but they weren't very deep. "To really understand classical," she said one weekend afternoon, "you must listen to Bach, Beethoven, and Mozart." I was extremely impressed by her knowledge and her music collection, and I sat in her room on Saturday afternoons trying to understand this music that was so new to me. But it was a little like going to a

French restaurant and ordering *escargot*. I liked it all right and
appreciated a new experience. But to be honest, I preferred the
cheeseburgers at Hamburger Heaven. The "cheeseburgers" of
my music world were composers like Bill Haley and the Com-
ets, Chubby Checkers and The Four Tops. I liked music that
you could get up and move to, not just sit and listen to. It
seemed to me that the only people who could move to Mozart
were serious ballerinas who had studied dance for years. For
me, movement wasn't about being serious or in control. When
I danced, I gave myself permission to push beyond the prim
boundaries of my upbringing and enter into a primal, wild
place that I intuitively knew I needed to set free.

I began to question things I had always taken for granted.
Big things, like the existence of God, and if there was a God,
who or what was God. My Christian beliefs were strong, and I
felt a great comfort when I prayed to Jesus, but I began to wonder about other practices. We studied about Buddhism in my
Philosophy class, and I became fascinated by its teachings and
the concept of reincarnation. I liked the idea of the soul coming back for many lifetimes in order to evolve, and the inter-
connectedness of Spirit resonated for me. I began to think of
God as more than a father figure who judged His children from
on high. In my mind, God was still gender specific, but I had
begun to explore my relationship with Him in a different way.
Rather than being outside of me and far away, I started to feel
the oneness of a Spirit that was in all things and everywhere.

One of the requirements for graduation was to write a
thirty-page paper on a subject of our choice. Before I began, I
went to see the headmistress for her approval of my topic. "So
Lisa," she said, smiling crookedly at me, "what are you going to
write about?" Even though I was one of the Heads of School,
and had been involved in many leadership activities during

my three years there, I had the feeling this woman didn't really like me.

"Well," I answered her nervously, "I want to write about reincarnation and call the paper *The Wheel of Rebirth*." I looked at her face and thought I detected an expression of patronizing amusement.

"That's a very large subject. Do you think you're up to it?" she replied, reaching for a cigarette. Then she added, "You will need to do a lot of research, and I am not sure that the school library has enough books on the subject."

"Are you saying I should choose another topic?"

"No, I'm just warning you. It won't be easy, and you do want to get a good grade, even though you're not going to college." She glanced at me with what could only be described as a look of dismissal, so I told her I'd work hard and left her office.

It was a raw March day, and while I walked through the quad to my room, I thought about what she had said. The words "even though you're not going to college" kept repeating themselves in my head. I felt ashamed that I wasn't going, but I believed I wasn't smart enough. I knew my only option was a junior college and that going to one would be much the same as two more years of boarding school. I had loved it, but I couldn't imagine still living with all those rules until I was twenty. When Mummy and I had discussed my future, it seemed to make sense that I go back to New York, enroll in Interior Design school, and live at home with her. She had pointed out that going to design school would teach me something practical that I could use in life. I loved the idea of decorating, and since Mummy had assured me that I had very good taste, I decided design school, not college, was the right choice. I also knew Mummy wouldn't feel so lonely if I was living back at home.

I worked hard researching and writing *The Wheel of Rebirth* and learned a lot about a world I had known absolutely nothing about. I loved the assignment because the choice to study Buddhism and reincarnation was my own. It was a study that came from some place inside me longing for change and new direction, the part of me that was beginning to step outside the box and question the status quo.

My graduation in June 1963, just a few days before my eighteenth birthday, was a gorgeous, shiny, clear "Maine Day," in Connecticut. The apple trees in the quad had bloomed a few weeks earlier but there were still a few blossoms scattered on the branches now covered in new bright green leaves. It was an exciting day, with touches of melancholy falling around us like the old blossoms. I was ready to leave the institution, but not my friends. We had sung and prayed in chapel, played sports, acted in plays, studied, gossiped, eaten three meals a day, and brushed our teeth together every night for three years.

Aside from saying goodbye to everyone, the day was perfect, and one of the things that made it so was that my parents, Lee, and I were together again, as a family. We were a "looking good" family. I knew that every teenage female eye was watching Daddy, and looking at me with envy. Daddy was wearing the madras jacket and yellow linen pants he had worn to parties in Maine. His black eye patch added an air of mystery to an otherwise classically handsome preppy look. Mummy looked lovely. Over her dress she wore a new cashmere sweater with appliquéd flowers sewn on the cuffs and down the front. Her hair had recently been frosted, and streaks of blond glimmered in the sun. I knew that it meant a lot to her to look as pretty as she could that day. My brother, nearly fourteen, was turning into a handsome young man. He looked very grown up in his navy blue blazer and red and blue striped tie. His hair was still blond, and he had added hair tonic to slick it down so it wouldn't have the normal tousled look. The only one in my family who didn't look good was me. One of the traditions at my school that I hated was having to wear our ugly white uniforms on our graduation day. Even on our last day together, it was important that everyone look the same. We did wear our cranberry-colored senior blazers over the uniform, so they gave us a little color.

Our senior class was the first class to graduate in the brand new gym that had been completed at the beginning of the year. Even though the day was beautiful and a ceremony outside would have been much nicer, the headmistress, who was retiring and whom the gym was named after, insisted that we hold the graduation inside.

I always felt emotional when I heard the march "Pomp and Circumstance" that is so often played at graduation ceremonies, and I knew that once we started filing into the gym, I'd probably be overwhelmed and cry. I was in the front of the line holding our class banner with the other four Heads of School, and all sixty girls were lined up behind us. When we heard the music, we began the procession into the gym. We were partway down the aisle, stepping in rhythm to the march, when the new PA system stopped dead and the strains of the sentimental "Pomp and Circumstance" ended in a scratchy crackle. I panicked for a moment. Then I felt angry. How could this be happening? Without the march, our perfect graduation moment would be spoiled. It had been bad enough not being able to wear a beautiful white graduation dress, and now our class didn't have music to march in to. Then, from behind me I heard a soft humming, and a moment later it got louder and I realized it was the clear and confident sound of my classmates singing the graduation march we all knew so well. Our voices joined together and became the beautiful music that guided us down the aisle and into the beginning of our new lives. It was one of the loveliest moments of the day and brought tears of pride and affection to my eyes. When I had received my diploma and sat down, I looked over the crowd to find my parents and Lee. They were in the fourth row sitting together, smiling and clapping. My family was together again, and I thought for just an instant that my prayers in the chapel had been answered, the divorce had never happened, and everything was still the same.

Three days later Daddy took me and a few of my friends from school to the Stork Club to celebrate my eighteenth birthday. The Stork Club was considered to be one of Manhattan's swankiest dinner clubs. It was very glamorous and bore no resemblance to the African Room, whatsoever. Small round tables circled a tiny dance floor, and larger tables with banquettes covered in red velvet were placed around the perimeter of the room. We all squeezed together on one of the banquettes, and after we were settled, Daddy joked, "I feel like I have a harem!" I felt very grown up in my little black dress, and I wore the diamond earrings that had been my grandmother's and were a gift from Mummy. That afternoon I had gone to Elizabeth Arden's to get rid of my bubble hair style that I had had for the last several years. At eighteen I was ready for something less cute and more sophisticated.

Daddy ordered champagne. After it arrived and the waiter had poured us each a glass, Daddy raised his to toast me: "To my wonderful daughter Lisa on turning eighteen. I wish you every happiness, all my love, and special congratulations because now you can drink—legally!" Then he laughed and winked at me. It never occurred to me then that drinking wouldn't always be something to celebrate.

DEBUTANTE

I AM HALFWAY THROUGH MY story and I need to stop for a moment and take a break from my adolescence. Endeavoring to write the truth of who I was in the sixties has been a bit daunting, at least from the perspective of who I am now. Of course it does little good to go back to the past and wish you could change it, but there are certain things that if I could do over again, I would. For instance, I might have chosen not to drink. I could have found work being of service in my community. I might have left home with a backpack and toured the world, or decided to join the civil rights march in Selma. But, in hindsight, I can see that any departure from the norm would have been impossible. The "good girl" didn't have time to consider becoming "the rebel." I believed I had to stay in a role that was familiar and safe because my parents were dealing with life-threatening illnesses and they needed me. Now, as I look back on that decision, I can easily see that it was probably the only choice I ever truly had. Aside from thinking of my family, I understand that I wasn't mature or consciously evolved enough to climb out of the security of my self-imposed box and peer over the edge. I might have found myself in a larger life if I had.

Instead, as I approached the end of adolescence, my life appears to have gotten somewhat out of control.

After my graduation from boarding school in June 1963, the swirl of debutante parties began and continued until the New Year. I had barely gotten my school trunk unpacked when I left with friends to travel up and down the East Coast attending large debutante dances. I had friends who lived in Virginia, Pennsylvania, Connecticut, and Washington, D.C., and they had invited hundreds of guests to their coming-out parties held in enormous white tents set up on beautifully manicured lawns. At many of the parties we danced to society's best dance bands, Lester Lanin, and Meyer Davis. My friends' parents had to sign these particular musicians up the year their daughters were born, for a party eighteen years later. If they had sons, the list they put their newborn *boys* names on were for enrollment at Harvard, Princeton, or Yale.

Mummy and I had shopped long hours during my spring vacation for summer evening dresses. After we made our selections, we bought several pairs of inexpensive white silk pumps and had them dyed to match each dress. Before I left on my debutante tour Mummy helped me pack my dresses and shoes, folding the dresses in tissue and arranging them carefully in my new red suitcase. Once we were ready, three friends and I drove out of the city in Mummy's Peugot station wagon and headed south for Virginia.

For several weeks, I ate, drank, and danced my way up the East coast. There were many mornings when I'd watch the sun rise, then go sleep for the rest of the day. All the dances had open bars and no one ever checked an ID. These were private parties. The bars were well stocked with half-gallon bottles of every kind of alcohol, lined up in rows like soldiers on the front lines. Waiters in black pants and short white jackets stood behind each table ready to mix whatever drink you asked for. At one party there was a fountain continuously gushing a waterfall of champagne. It sat on its own special table with champagne glasses surrounding it. All you had to do was pick up a glass, hold it under the fountain, and fill it up. After drinking all night, kids got into cars and drove to wherever they were staying. No one, not even the parents, seemed concerned about it. By the end of June I was beginning to hear about car crashes, some of them fatal.

I had discovered that I could hold my liquor really well. Sometimes it felt like I had what people called "a hollow leg." I felt proud of this ability. I was glad that drinking didn't make me act sloppy or stupid. Even when I drank, I knew it was important to try and keep up with appearances.

Toward the end of the first month of parties, I met a really good-looking guy named Todd who told me he was a member of the "Shock Troopers." I had heard about this roving band of bad boys and was both titillated and frightened by the stories. There were six of them, all in their twenties, and extremely handsome. They had dropped out of college, and it seemed as though the jobs they had were going to debutante dances, invited or otherwise. I had no idea what they did for work. Maybe they were trust fund babies too. They each had the look of a well-heeled WASP. They wore the right clothes and had the right hairstyles, but I suspected that they were imposters. Their having nearly legitimized the image attracted me even more, and I imagined that they were the Gatsby's of my generation. I had realized a while ago that I kind of liked bad boys. Maybe they reminded me of Daddy.

I suppose I was beginning to feel a bit bored by the debutante routine and the fact that the parties were all pretty much the same. Since most of my good friends had gone home by then, I took Todd up on his invitation to travel with him and crash a big party in Washington, D.C. Unfortunately, the party we crashed was being given by a girl I had gone to elementary school with but hadn't seen for several years. She recognized me and knew I hadn't been invited. Todd and I left quickly, the same way we arrived, under the tent, before her parents were informed. The Shock Troopers had acquired a rather unsavory reputation and were beginning to be recognized. The bouncers were on the alert.

"Where will we go now, Todd?" I ask him as we pull out of the driveway in Mummy's car. I am feeling naughty, and I don't entirely dislike the feeling. It sure beats the proverbial "good girl" image that has been expected of me and I have worked so hard to perfect.

"I live near here," he answers me. "We can go there and spend the night." Now I am beginning to worry that I haven't thought this through very well. I have had too much to drink, a guy I barely know is driving my mother's car, and he is taking me to a Shock Trooper house. When we get to his house there are a lot of people there, drinking and making out. I don't know anyone, and I am very tired and nervous.

"Where can I sleep, Todd? I need to go to bed."

"Oh, you can sleep with me. There aren't any free rooms. We're full tonight," he adds with what I presume to be a leer. I have no idea how I have gotten myself into this predicament, but I am too exhausted to figure it out. Tomorrow I'll be driving to Pennsylvania to attend my best friend's party, and I can leave all this behind me. Before I lie down on the bed, I open my suitcase, remove the lacey pink curler bag, and set my hair in wire mesh rollers, haphazardly attaching them to my head with bobby pins. My hair isn't very clean, but at least it will be curly. Then I stretch out on the double bed, fully clothed, and pass out. Later that night when Todd comes to bed, he doesn't touch me. Thankfully, he's had too much to drink too and passes out beside me. The next morning, I wake up early to a strange and unfamiliar scene, and I realize that I don't like feeling naughty anymore. I quickly pack, leave the house, and drive away before he wakes up. I never saw him or any other Shock Troopers again.

One of biggest, splashiest parties was in Southampton, Long Island, at the end of June. It was given by a very wealthy family that was definitely "old money." I didn't know the debutante, but Mummy explained that my name was on a list and that sometimes with the really big private parties they had to acquire extra names so there would be enough guests.

"But we do have a connection, sweetie," Mummy told me while we sat together in the living room one night enjoying a cocktail together. "Fernanda's mother and I went to school together in Philadelphia. Of course that was years ago, but those are the kinds of associations that can really help later on. Also, if we weren't in the Social Register, I doubt you would have received an invitation." The Social Register is a little black book, published in many cities every year. It is filled with the names and addresses of society's older families. To be in it is considered by some to be extremely prestigious.

"The Social Register is just a convenience," Mummy had always told me. "You don't have to wade through the phone book, and it is so nice that they include maiden names and where the men went to college." I remembered one time when I was younger, Mummy got very upset with me when she overheard me asking a friend from school if she was in the Social

Register. "It might make her feel bad, Lisa," she explained. "Many people want to get in to the Social Register, but they just aren't eligible. We don't want to call attention to that fact or take it for granted." I was not sure that I really understood, but I was definitely given the impression that the Social Register was an important little book.

I declined the invitation in Southampton because I had been invited by one of my friends from school to a house-party weekend at the Homestead, a glamorous old-world hotel resort in the hills of West Virginia. They were chartering an airplane large enough to fly many of the guests down, and for the dance Saturday night, they had booked a new rock and roll singing group named The Pointer Sisters to entertain us.

A few days after I arrived back home from West Virginia, I got a phone call from a friend. "Oh my God, Lisa, have you heard what happened at Fernanda's party?"

"That party in Southampton? No, I am kind of sorry I didn't go."

"Well, it's lucky you didn't, you might have ended up in jail."

"What on earth do you mean?"

"Kids went crazy at the after-party. The guest house was opened up for people to continue partying, and lots of them got really drunk. They were swinging like Tarzan from crystal chandeliers and ripped them right out of the ceiling, and then they threw furniture out the windows onto the beach. The place was a real mess when the police finally came and arrested them all."

I was beginning to understand that this was really serious, and that I was damn lucky not to have been there. "What happened? Did they go to jail?" I asked my friend.

"Yeah, some of them, mostly boys. I didn't know any of them who were booked. But maybe you do?"

Two days later, the weekly issue of *LIFE* magazine was on the newsstands. On the cover in a line-up with I D cards and

numbers around their necks were the twenty kids who had
been arrested at the party. They had sobered up, and no one
looked like they were having fun anymore. "But they did make
the cover of *LIFE* magazine," someone joked. Inside there was
a really embarrassing story about "wealthy society kids," and
when I saw the picture, I realized I knew two of the boys in the
line-up. I had gone to dancing school with one, and the other
was my Shock Trooper friend Todd.

After the June season was over, three of my school friends and
I stayed in my apartment and went to work at summer jobs. I
had a job working at my old friend Stevee's father's fabric show-
room, which was perfect since I'd be going to Interior Design
School in the fall. My mother and brother had gone to Maine,
so we had the apartment to ourselves. In two months' time I
got fat eating deli sandwiches from the Hole in the Wall Deli
and drinking pitchers of daiquiris. When my mother arrived
home from Maine at the end of the summer, she was horrified
by the way I looked. I was going to be "presented" to society in
just three short months, and it certainly would not do to have a
fat debutante in the family. I was 130 pounds and it was a crisis.
So I joined my mother's fear of shaming the family with fat and
went along willingly when she said we were going to see a well-
known East Side diet doctor.

"Of course I can help you," Dr. M. smiles generously at us
both. I notice that his black hair has a sheen that looks like my
father's wing tips after he has applied liberal amounts of black
shoe polish, and that he has a sharp, bird-like nose and cold,
hard eyes. As I watch him standing there in his stiffly starched
white doctor's coat, I know that I don't like this man. But if he

can promise that I'll lose twenty pounds in time for my debutante party in December, I don't have to like him.

"We'll do whatever you say," Mummy chimes in as I nod vigorously.

Every week that fall after my design classes, I take the Lexington Avenue bus uptown to get a shot of diuretics in the fanny and a fresh supply of green, pink, blue, and red pills that are stuffed into a small white box. I swallow one of each every day before meals. I have no idea what I am swallowing, and I don't care. All I know is that I am feeling great—better than great. I am soaring on speed. High on uppers, chain smoking, and best of all, I could care less about food. But what I love most is that for the first time in my life, Mummy isn't criticizing me about eating too much or eating the wrong foods. I am barely eating anything, and we are both happy because my weight is "under control."

In hindsight, I wish with all my heart I had not betrayed myself and had told my mother there was no reason to pop pills to get thin. I wish that I had had the courage to tell her my body belonged to me, not her, and that I wasn't fat at 130 pounds. If I had only loved myself enough in that moment, I think my relationship with my body as an adult might have been different.

By mid-November I am ready. I weigh 112 pounds, and at the final fitting for my debutante dress, the seamstress at Saks has to take the waist in another inch. This is my special dress, the one I will wear to my own party in December, but Mummy and

I have also picked out several other gowns for the various balls that I'll be going to during the season. We have bought a few pairs of elbow-length white kid gloves, and Mummy has given me an early Christmas present, a bolero style, pale mink jacket, to keep me warm. "Pale mink is more youthful and suitable than dark mink for someone your age, dearie," Mummy tells me when I try it on.

Because I wasn't away at college but living at home, I was able to please my mother and give the holiday debutante season my undivided attention. I put my foot down, however, when I was asked to be part of a choreographed dance for the Debutante Cotillion at the Waldorf Astoria Hotel. After two rehearsals parading across a stage on the arm of some boy in a military uniform that I didn't even know, holding a giant green ostrich-feather fan and curtsying deeply to the other girls who were holding fans too, I knew I couldn't be part of this pageant. I had some pride. Actually, I was beginning to feel confused about the frivolous role of debutante. All my friends were away at college, and it seemed as though the girls who weren't in college, and therefore thought not to be very smart, were the ones being "used" for this pretense. I definitely did not want to be part of that image. But I loved the glamour, the mystique of the balls in the beautiful ballrooms, the dresses, the handsome boys in their dinner jackets. Somehow I knew none of it held any real importance, but I never considered turning my back on it.

I was looking forward to seeing my friends over Thanksgiving when they came home from college. Living at home and going to design school was turning out to be lonely. After three years of boarding school, I missed the constant companionship of friends my own age, and I did not appreciate being told by Mummy to pick my clothes up off the floor or that it was late and I should stop watching television and go to bed. I was practically an adult, after all.

Easter 1948

Top left: Betty and Bev—
1940.
Top right: author, 1945.
Right: four generations,
Greatie, Gommy, Daddy
and me.
Bottom left: with Nanny
and Papa in Maine and
Mummy, awaiting
brother Lee.
Bottom right: Lee, 1953.

Betty, Bev, Lisa and Lee in Maine—1955

Debutante, with Mummy and Lee, 1963

Peter in Maine—1978

The kids and me in Maine—1986

Elise and Hugh's wedding with Barstow family—1995

Bill and me in Kauai—2005

Grand children Alex, Jonathan, Allison Sweet—2008

Grandchildren Leila and Henry Gaasch—2008

Sabrina, Elise and Adrian Mott—2008

The amphetamines kept me high and disinterested in food for most of the day, but the cravings started when I was alone in my room at night. There were many nights when I needed that extra midnight sandwich to fill up the hole that my loneliness was carving inside me. I began to feel frightening and unfamiliar emotions. I was experiencing disquieting feelings of discontent and disconnection that I would now describe as a separation from self. I experienced a sense of myself splitting in two, not knowing which part was the real me. Although it was difficult to put into words then, I wrote about it in my diary but never told anyone. I had learned that it was best to keep my feelings to myself. They weren't nearly as dire as cancer, adultery, or divorce. Besides, if I tried not to think about what was going on inside, it would probably go away.

It was during this time of unease that Peter Mott came back into my life. His presence was timely and helped distract me from my depression. I felt more stable when I was with him because he was stable. I was naïve, however, to think I could glean something I needed from someone other than myself.

Peter's family were old friends of my family, and although he had come to my birthday parties when we were young, we hadn't seen each other for fifteen years. I have a photograph of him at my fifth birthday. It was a costume party and he came dressed as a cowboy. He is looking shyly at the camera, standing separately from the group. Most everyone else was from my kindergarten class, but he had been invited because our mothers were friends.

I had a crush on him. He wasn't rough or tough like the other boys I knew. I remember being drawn to his shyness, his thick brown curls, and the bursts of freckles on his cheek bones and nose. He was always dressed formally, even in the neighborhood park we played in, and my mother would comment that it was a shame that Peter didn't wear the kind of clothes to the playground that you didn't have to worry about getting dirty. As a result, this little boy always appeared to be holding himself in, without permission to just let loose and play hard.

When we re-met in 1963, we were both attending an old, established pre-Thanksgiving Ball in Tuxedo Park, New York. I was dancing with my friend Chris, complaining that I hardly knew anyone there:

"Do *you* know anyone here?" I ask him.

"No, not many, but I went to school with that guy over there," and he points to a nice-looking boy sitting at a table close to where we are dancing. "His name is Peter Mott."

"Oh, I used to know him," I reply, eying Peter with more interest. "He came to all my birthday parties when we were little. Our parents have been friends for years."

"Well, let me introduce you after all these years," Chris quips, as he leads me over to the table where Peter is sitting.

As we approach, Peter stands up, and before Chris has a chance to speak, he says, "You're Lisa Barstow, aren't you?" Then he gives me a big friendly smile, adding, "I know you."

I like him immediately, and although his eyes are a steel blue, they are warm and welcoming. He still has thick curls, but now they are slicked down with hair tonic. His demeanor still seems quite proper, and I realize he hasn't changed much from that formal six-year-old I had known. As a matter of fact, he could pass for someone from Britain, not New Jersey.

"Oh yes, I remember you too. How have you been?"

"Would you like to dance?" he replies instead of answering me, and when I nod, he takes my hand and leads me onto the dance floor. I wave goodbye to Chris, mouthing the words "thank you" over Peter's shoulder. As he takes me in his arms, I realize that he isn't very tall, probably 5'8" or so. I am just 5'3," and as we begin to dance, I can't help but notice how perfectly we fit together. I don't feel shy or self-conscious, like I usually do when I am dancing with someone I don't know. Peter is familiar, a childhood friend, and I am immediately at ease. He seems so sophisticated, so sure of himself. He tells me that he has just spent the summer working at the Morgan Bank in Paris, that his high school French has become fluent, and that he considers himself a "Francophile."

"I appreciate the culture there. The language is beautiful and so is the art. I am also very interested in the history. But what I love best about France is the food and the wine. Americans just don't know how to spend time eating and drinking with style." I am impressed that he would take such an adult job, and that he cares about culture, fine food, and wine. I realize that at twenty, he is very grown up, and I like that a lot. We dance and talk until the band plays "Good Night Ladies" and it is time to leave the Ball.

"I am so glad that we met again," he says softly as he reaches over and gives me a kiss on the cheek.

"Me too," I answer him, wishing I could think of something more interesting to say. I have just had one of the nicest times I have ever had with a boy, and I'm wondering when I will see him again.

As if reading my mind, Peter asks, "Would you like to come up to Trinity for Homecoming Weekend in two weeks? Now that I've found you again I don't want as many years to go by before we see each other again."

I say "yes" immediately.

Two weeks later, I go to Homecoming Weekend at Trinity College, and I am in love when I leave. This is my first college weekend, and I am amazed at how many people, mostly boys, get sloppy drunk at the fraternity parties. Peter has plenty to drink but he doesn't show it. He drinks like a gentleman and behaves that way too. We visit other frat parties that night, and I notice, with disgust, that I have to maneuver my way around smelly puddles of beer and cigarette butts on the floor. At one fraternity house, there are wads of gum floating in the beer or stuck to basement floor.

I'm not unhappy when Peter suggests that we leave the parties early and go back to the motel where he has booked a room for me. I have never stayed in a motel and although I am feeling a bit nervous, I am reassured when Peter tells me it is where all the girls stay. After he parks the car and goes into the office to get the room key, he grabs my overnight case and walks with me up the stairs to the second level that looks out over the parking lot. He unlocks the door and we go in. I scan the room with my newly trained decorator's eye and I don't like what I see. The room has a double bed with a plastic headboard, pretending to be wood, a brown and olive-green quilted spread, and a drab picture over the bed. It is a print of an autumn landscape, painted in dull greens and dingy oranges, the colors of fall after the peak.

I am staring at the bed when Peter walks over and takes me in his arms. Then he kisses me. We inch our way over to the bed and lie down side by side. The spread smells like cigarettes, and the bright white ceiling is rough and bumpy. We kiss and touch each other for a long time on top of the spread, and although I hope he will stay, he doesn't spend the night.

When I get home on Sunday afternoon, I discuss the weekend with Mummy. "Peter was a perfect gentleman," I tell her.

"I wouldn't have expected anything less from him," she says. "The fact that he said there is plenty of time is wonderful, sweetie, because it sounds as though he's committing to something more than just a weekend fling." I feel happy and reassured by this conversation with Mummy. I have been her confidante about Daddy, and more recently about some of the men she's dating. Now, she can be mine about Peter.

It is toward the end of November, and I have gotten home after morning classes at design school. I grab some lunch and decide to turn on my favorite soap opera, *Days of our Lives*. The television is in Lee's room. After he left for boarding school in September, Mummy and I redecorated his room to make it more sophisticated. The painter came and scraped the soldier wallpaper off the walls and painted them a light green. The bed became a day bed with a fitted dark green spread and lots of throw pillows, and instead of a linoleum floor, Mummy bought a beige wool rug. "Now this room looks like a den instead of a little boy's room," Mummy announced proudly once it was done.

I am curled up on the day bed, and while I eat my sandwich I am absorbed into the ongoing drama of my soap. Then a news bulletin flashes across the T.V. screen. "What now?" I grumble to myself, annoyed that I'll have to wait a minute before I find out if Betty is going to ditch Neil or not.

**STAND BY FOR AN IMPORTANT
ANNOUNCEMENT—
PRESIDENT KENNEDY HAS BEEN SHOT IN DALLAS.**

Walter Cronkite comes on, looking very somber. My heart begins to beat fast. Surely the president will be all right. The newsman is telling us that President Kennedy has been rushed to the hospital. That his motorcade was fired on, and that they are awaiting more information. As I sit there, alone and terrified, I remembered going to Washington for the inauguration a few years earlier with a friend of mine from school who lives there. We watched the parade from an office building on the route, and I felt so proud of our new president and his beautiful Jackie, whom everyone in my family loved even though she was married to a Democrat. "She has brought class and culture back to our country," my grandmother Gommy told me.

Just then, the network shows a horrible picture of Jackie with blood all over her clothes, walking into the hospital. *This can't be happening,* I think and begin to cry. A few minutes later: "We have a confirmed report," Cronkite is telling us with tears rolling down his cheeks, **"PRESIDENT KENNEDY IS DEAD."**

This isn't real, it can't be real. I am stunned. Just then I hear the front door open and I rush into the hall. Mummy is home. I throw myself into her arms and tell her what has happened. She and I walk into Lee's room, sit down on the bed, and watch the horrible story, hugging each other, and crying hard for our young president who has been assassinated just a few days before Thanksgiving.

Several hours later, I am standing in Grand Central Station waiting for the train to take me to New Haven for homecoming weekend at Yale. I don't know the boy I am going to visit very well, but I agreed to go several weeks before I met Peter again.

Leaving the protection of my apartment, and being in the middle of a very public place, brings the horror of what has just happened into clearer focus. People are walking around in a daze, many are crying, and others have formed small circles and are talking about the tragedy. Young boys are selling newspapers with the headline **PRESIDENT KENNEDY DEAD,** and the front page is bordered in black. I am reminded of pictures of newspapers in my U.S. history books when Lincoln was shot. I am overwhelmed with sadness. Minutes later, I go to a phone booth and call my friend at Yale.

"I can't come visit you," I tell him. "This is just so horrible."

"I know, all the parties have been canceled. But why don't you come anyway? I'd like to see you," he replies.

"No, I'm sorry, Drew, I just need to stay home. This is a lot to take in. I'll talk to you after Thanksgiving." As I walk through the enormous station to get a cab and go home, I look up and notice the huge Kodak color pictures that line the circular hall. They are photographs of happy families playing in piles of gold and orange leaves, and freckle-faced kids hugging white-haired grandparents who have come to visit for Thanksgiving. The best one is of a large smiling family seated around a dining room table laden with harvest foods, and at the head, the father is getting ready to carve an enormous turkey.

These are pictures of America, I think as I walk by. Then I imagine another picture, the one that the news stations are showing over and over on T.V. It's the one of the motorcade in Dallas with the president and his wife smiling and waving at the crowd. Then it cuts to one of terror as people along the route drop to their knees. There's Jackie in her blood-stained bright pink suit. Her matching pillbox hat is gone and her perfect hairdo is disheveled, with hair falling over her eyes. Now, I think sadly to myself, these images will be part of the American Thanksgiving picture as well.

The parties at Yale are not the only ones to be called off. All the debutante dances that were scheduled for Thanksgiving weekend are canceled as well. I am relieved. I cannot imagine getting dressed up and dancing when the country is in mourning. I was to have been presented at the Junior League Ball at the Plaza Hotel that weekend. It has been postponed and rescheduled for December 27th. The night of my party.

Now, Mummy and I are in the middle of what appears to be a social disaster. The invitations have been printed and are being addressed, the ballroom has been rented, and deposits have been sent to the caterer and the band. "We just can't change the date. Oh, what on earth are we going to do?" Mummy is in a state of high anxiety. I have no idea what we can do, but to me, none of this seems very important considering what has just happened to President Kennedy and his family.

By the following week, everything has been worked out. The League agrees to delay the Ball until eleven PM, allowing me and my parents at least four hours to entertain 100 family and friends for dinner and dancing.

A week before the party, Mummy and I are sitting in her bedroom talking. She is lying on the chaise, her favorite spot in the late afternoon. We are both sipping tea. She looks tired. She has been working hard putting finishing touches on the many details for the party and organizing Christmas at the same time. The phone rings, and she reaches over to answer it. It's Daddy.

"I have decided that I cannot attend the party unless Fritzi can come. She is my wife after all." He is speaking so loudly that I can hear his voice through the receiver.

"Bev," my mother replies, "I thought you understood that after all you have put us through, leaving us for that woman, I cannot have her in the same room with me on one of the most important nights of our daughter's life." Then Mummy hangs up the phone with a bang. She is beginning to scratch at her eczema, and I know it will be bleeding soon.

"What did he say?" I ask, pretending I hadn't heard the conversation.

"He said he won't come unless Fritzi comes with him, and we both know that is impossible."

I am sitting on the edge of the twin bed that used to be Daddy's, and for a moment I don't reply. I think about the times that Daddy, in deference to my mother, has shown up without his new wife: my graduation and my eighteenth birthday party; and I had found out that Mummy told him he could never come back to Maine with Fritzi because it was Mummy's summer home, not his. I am old enough to understand that Daddy feels guilty and has been trying to be fair to my mother. I also know that Mummy has not forgiven him. Once again I feel squeezed between the two of them and their needs, trying to help sort things out.

"What should we do, Lisa?" One thing I am clear about is that Mummy will never allow Fritzi to come to my debutante party.

"Well, if he won't go then I'm not going either." I pick up the phone and call my father's apartment to tell him of my decision.

"He says he'll think about it," I tell her when I get off the phone.

The next day, four days before Christmas and less than a week before my party, Daddy calls to say he has reconsidered. He will come without his wife.

When I began this book, the working title was *Confessions of a Debutante*, and several drafts later I changed it to *The Dance of the Debutante*. I thought that the word *Debutante* in the title would have neon lights attached to it while it sat on the bookstore shelves. What a clever marketing ploy, I told myself, feeling very pleased. As I kept writing, getting older and wiser at the same time, I began to realize that I didn't want my story to be identified as one written by a debutante. I thought about cutting this chapter altogether. After all, I had worked too hard to transcend those earlier, frivolous years. Then I read Rumi's poem and understood that life is a continual motion back and forth across the doorsill where the worlds of the conscious and the unconscious touch. I have awakened to believe that every event in our journey through each lifetime makes up the whole, and to judge any part of the experience is to negate who we have been and who we are becoming.

One of my best friends, whom I met in my early forties, could have been a debutante, but she chose to go work in the slums of Liverpool, England, instead. When I heard this, I immediately felt inferior. She had chosen to be in service to others when I was careening in and out of deb parties and their champagne fountains. Later on in our friendship, we laughed about the disparity of our lives when we were in our teens and marveled at how our "lives' journeys" had brought us together. She has helped me to see that no matter what choices I made in the moment, the important thing is that I haven't gone back to sleep. She sees the whole picture, and has pointed out that our experiences are on two sides of the same coin. Thank you, dear Nan.

My story would not be complete without acknowledging the debutante in me. She is an important part of who I was then, and she has helped me to become who I am now. Nonetheless, I am glad that I changed the title of my book.

My made-to-order dress was perfect for Christmastime. Sewn onto the neckline were small clusters of appliquéd green leaves and tiny red berries that looked like holly, and the white silk organza skirt had several sprigs scattered around for color. Even my white silk shoes had the holly attached to the sides.

"It's original," Mummy said after we had taken it out of the garment bag. She seemed very pleased about that.

I was still consuming diet pills, but because I had lost my weight Dr. M. had put me on a maintenance dose. I had become very attached to these tiny nuggets of speed. They insured me against the horror of fat. I could eat and drink whatever I liked, and I was still going to fit into my dress. This gave me, and Mummy, some real peace of mind.

I had asked Peter to be my escort at my party and for the Junior League Ball afterwards. In the two months between the Tuxedo Ball in early November and now, we had fallen in love. My feelings for him were completely different than the ones I had had for summer boyfriends, or the serious romance I'd had with a boy I met over spring break in Bermuda my junior year. This was real and felt adult, like Peter.

The dinner dance was held at The Georgian Suite, a small, intimate ballroom tucked away on the ground floor of an apartment building in the 70's between Madison and Fifth. When I stepped into the vestibule and saw the room for the first time I gasped at how enchanting it was. Mummy had transformed the rather unadorned ballroom into a celebration of holiday light and color. Strings of tiny white lights sparkled as they wove through garlands of feathery greenery and curled around miniature boxwood trees that stood at the center of each of the ten round tables. The tables were covered with white damask cloths and thick strands of deep pink satin ribbon trailed across the diameters. A few anemones, pink to match the ribbons, were nestled like ornaments in each of the boxwood trees. The waiters had folded the bright pink cloth napkins like fans and placed one on each of the gold-rimmed white plates. Small white place cards, trimmed in gold, were beside each place setting.

"Oh Mummy," I exclaim, "it looks like a fairy land. This is more beautiful than I could have ever dreamed it would be. Thank you so much." Before I go over to give my mother a hug, I spend a moment and really look at her. She is lovely. Despite having to organize almost all of this herself, she looks happy and serene. Her long satin strapless sheath compliments her slim figure, and the blend of different colors of green is very becoming. Her brown hair has fresh blond streaks in it, and whatever hairspray she used has worked, giving her hair the much-desired thickness and stillness. This is not the time for hair to look unkempt.

"You look beautiful, Mummy," I tell her warmly.

"And so do you, dearie," she says returning the compliment. I know she is being sincere. I do look beautiful. My dress is gorgeous, my hair has been teased and curled, my green eyes are shining like the diamond earrings I am wearing, my makeup is not too much but just enough, and I am thin.

Daddy arrives escorting his mother instead of his wife and proceeds through the evening graciously as the co-host with Mummy. They sit at separate tables, however. Lee, wearing a tuxedo for the first time, looks so grown up and handsome. At fourteen he is definitely debonair. He has learned well.

Before my friends arrive, the band that Daddy hired walks in and begins to set up. My father thought that instead of the formal debutante band, it would be more fun to have a jazz band, and he had heard about a great black jazz band from Baltimore. The musicians are wearing bright red tuxedo jackets with matching bowties and black pants. Daddy jokes around with the bandleader whose name is Rivers Chambers, and the minute they begin to play I know that it will be a fabulous party.

It's odd, but I have no recollection of what was served for dinner.

Daddy comes over to ask me for the first dance, and we two-step vigorously around the room with everyone watching us. Then, after a few moments, Peter cuts in, and everyone else gets up to dance. In that moment I feel like Cinderella at the Ball.

SUMMERS IN EUROPE

THE SUMMER THAT DADDY LEFT, I turned fifteen, drank my first beer, and went to second base. I was told by my best friend's father that I was boy crazy, but I didn't care. Maine was a safe place to experiment growing up. My boyfriends were the sons of my parents' friends, and most of the beers we consumed were in front of bonfires at beach parties that were within walking distance of home. I had my driver's license, gas was 25 cents a gallon, and my mother let me borrow her car whenever I wanted. My girlfriends and I drove around all day listening to the top hits and chain smoking. It was the early sixties, a time before seat belts and DUI's, and there were evenings when our group would drive back from a bar in town, feet sticking out of windows, taking the curves at top speed, drunk.

The next summer, 1962, I had an invitation from a friend of mine in New York, an all-expense-paid, two-week trip cruising the Mediterranean on a private 175-foot yacht. "Tell them no," I pouted when Mummy asked me if I'd like to go. "I just want to be in Maine with my friends." Summers in Maine were all I knew and all I wanted to experience. I had no interest in leaving my familiar cocoon.

Fortunately, my mother was wise enough to decide for me. "You cannot pass up an opportunity like this," she told me. "It is incredibly kind of them to invite you and pay for you. I am accepting their generous invitation. You will be going on the cruise."

Mummy and I shopped for the trip like the veteran shoppers we were, and when I got on the plane, I was dressed in a beige and navy Peck and Peck cotton suit with navy blue pumps and a navy patent leather bag. I had a ticket for a seat in the first-class cabin, and before we took off, the stewardess asked me if I'd like some champagne. (I guess there's no drinking age in first class.) Later on the stewardess served me a delicious dinner, and for dessert I helped myself to several pastries, presented on a silver tray. I felt very grown up, and I had already decided that my mother was right. Going to Europe, all expenses paid, was not a bad way to spend a few weeks.

As the plane headed toward Italy, I began to wonder how Mummy would do without me there to talk to, but the stewardess interrupted my thoughts: "May I fill up your glass?" she asked, holding a bottle of French champagne.

"Oh yes, thank you," I replied with a somewhat sloppy grin. After two glasses I was feeling quite dizzy. *Must be the altitude*, I thought to myself as I snuggled under the grey wool blanket and drifted off to sleep. Several hours later, the plane landed in Rome and a car and driver met me at the airport. Then we drove south to Pisa, where I was to meet the rest of the group that had arrived several days earlier.

Everyone seemed very happy to see me and thought it was very funny that they were meeting "Leeza in Peeza." After a tour of the Leaning Tower, we drove the short distance to Livorno, a small port on the Mediterranean Sea, and boarded the *Miranda*, a 175-foot yacht that would take ten of us passengers, the British captain, and ten in the crew from the Italian Riviera to the French Riviera, then on to the Costa Brava in Spain.

"Oh Holly," I told my friend as we explored the decks. "I've never been on a boat this large. It is the most beautiful ship I have ever seen." There was a huge lounge with overstuffed sofas upholstered in cream-colored linen, mahogany tables, and a bar that looked like it came out of the Oak Room at the Plaza Hotel. The wood-paneled dining room had a table in it that could seat fourteen, and on the aft deck there was an outdoor living room and another bar. Every guest or couple had their own individual staterooms and their own personal bathroom, or head, as bathrooms are called on boats. I noticed that all the brass railings were polished to a bright shine that gleamed in the Mediterranean sun. The teak decks were spotless, as were the white uniforms on the captain and crew. When we arrived on board, they all lined up to greet us; one crew member for every guest. I noticed right away that one of them was just a few years older than me, and very cute, and I began to fantasize that the captain would see to it that he was assigned to me. Holly and I were the only teenagers on board. The other eight passengers were friends of Holly's parents, and after our first meeting, I could tell that I was going to enjoy spending time with them.

After the tour of the boat, there were just a few minutes to wash up before it was time to join everyone outside on the aft deck for a delicious buffet lunch with the captain. We ate antipasto, spaghetti tossed in olive oil with freshly grated parmesan, warm rolls, and melon. The captain told us things about the *Miranda* that we needed to know in case of an emergency, and about the route we'd be taking and the harbors we'd be visiting.

"Our first stop will be Portofino," the captain said. "We will be leaving momentarily and will dock in time for dinner. Cocktails will be served on the aft deck, and dinner is in the dining room. Enjoy your first afternoon at sea." Then he left to go to the bridge. A few minutes later I watched as one of the crew untied and cast off the lines, and two others removed the gangplank, stowing it away. I heard the engines rev, and a horn blew three times as the *Miranda* gracefully pushed away from the dock, heading for her first "port of call."

I didn't want to miss anything, so as we approached Portofino, I went up on the bow. I was enchanted by what I saw. It didn't look real. Before the European gentry discovered it, this had been a tiny, quaint fishing village used solely by fishermen, bringing in the catch of the day. Now those fishing boats had been replaced by large, fancy yachts like ours. The town curved around the harbor, forming a square, and shops and cafés were lined around the perimeter. I noticed how old the buildings looked painted in fading colors of mustard and burnt orange, with plaster walls that had long cracks running down them like snakes. Although they were old, the houses were bright and cheerful, with summer flowers blooming in boxes at every window. Some of them had grown so full they spilled out of the window boxes, cascading down the cracked walls.

I remembered that when Mummy had arrived home after her first trip to Europe two years earlier, she had told me, "Oh Lisa, Europe is so *picturesque*." I didn't know what she meant then, but looking at this Italian town I understood the meaning of the word *picturesque*. Then, in the midst of this exciting new adventure, I felt an overwhelming sadness for my mother, and tears began to run down my cheeks into the corners of my mouth. I licked them away and wiped my eyes with my arm. Mummy had been so happy and hopeful when she and Daddy decided to go to Europe together. Now Mummy was in Maine, still in love with Daddy, and I was the one in Italy.

After we docked and took a quick walking tour of Portofino, we went back to the boat for dinner. The adults discussed

politics and fascinating travel adventures to places like Egypt
and the Arctic, where they had met Eskimos. Holly and I were
included in the conversation and were asked for our opinions.
I found myself eagerly joining the discussion and realized I was
not sure I had ever been asked to give my opinion before. (Our
family dinners held conversations that were usually about table
manners and other people.) There was also an endless supply
of humor, thanks to a jovial red-faced man named Colonel
Fitzroy, Fritz for short, with droopy jowls and a cue-ball bald
head. Holly and I called him the Colonel.

A few days later, we left Italian waters and sailed into Mo-
naco on the French Riviera. The captain needed to use the
space reserved for Onassis's enormous yacht *Christina* because
the *Miranda* was too large for the average-size berths at the
dock. Holly, the Colonel, and I were standing on the deck as
the boat glided into the harbor of the small principality, where
one of my favorite movie stars, Grace Kelly, was Princess. I had
seen all her movies, and when she and Prince Ranier were married, I cut the pictures of their fairytale wedding out of *LIFE*
magazine and scotch-taped them to my bedroom wall, feeling
a little bit sorry that her prince wasn't younger and better looking. Now, I could see the palace sitting up on the hillside just
above the town, and I imagined Princess Grace swishing around
her bedroom in a lace negligee. The bedroom probably had a
huge canopy bed and large windows looking out on the sap-
phire blue sea.

"There's the Casino," the Colonel tells us, interrupting my
Grace Kelly reverie. He is pointing to an ornate, golden building that looks much fancier than the palace. "We will all be
going there tonight to gamble. Make sure to dress up and look

as old as you can." His eyes are twinkling mischievously. That evening our group disembarks to have dinner at an elegant restaurant on the quay, and afterwards we proceed to the steps of the historic Casino.

"Before we go in," Colonel Fitzroy explains, looking at one of the other men in our party, "Lisa and Holly will have to pretend to be our wives. You cannot get in to gamble if you're under eighteen, so maybe a wedding ring will convince the bouncer at the door that our young ladies are of age." Holly's mother and another woman remove their wedding rings and we put them on. We can't stop giggling, which isn't very adult. I am really glad that I put makeup on and am wearing my most sophisticated dress, a hot-pink cotton sheath with white polka dots, hemmed just above the knee. We all climb the steps to the entrance with its towering gilded wood doors. The bouncer is dressed in a tuxedo and stares at Holly and me as we are shuffled along on the arms of our "husbands." "*Ma femme,*" the Colonel says, as he grabs my left hand and shows him the wedding ring. I am standing up very straight, trying to look smooth and worldly, and *voilà!* we quickly glide through and into the Casino, leaving a skeptical French bouncer at the door.

Once inside, I am transfixed by the scene. The rooms are enormous, with ceilings at least thirty feet high and lights that look like hundreds of tiny candles shimmering on crystal chandeliers. Turn-of-the-century murals showing scenes of an elegant, old-world Monte Carlo lifestyle are painted on the walls, and French needlepoint rugs cover the marble floors. Because I am not the least bit *au courant* about gambling I have no idea what everyone is doing at the many gaming tables set up around the rooms. I recognize a roulette wheel, and for a while Holly and I watch the players stare at the wheel spinning round and around. They all look very intense, holding cigarettes and drinks in their hands. The Colonel asks if we want to test our luck, and I jump right in with the francs he hands me. Of course my number never comes up, and I soon tire of roulette, moving on to watch *chemin de fer* and the activity at the craps table. Actually, I am more interested in watching people than playing, so I roam around the Casino until it is time to leave. Once we are back on the boat, the grownups open bottles of champagne, and Holly and I are asked to join the party. It is a perfect way to end an elegant evening.

"You may have a little if you like, dear," Holly's mother tells me as the steward pours me a glass.

Well, it's not as though I have never had champagne before, I think as I take a glass filled with Dom Perignon. By the time Holly and I have said goodnight and gone to our stateroom, I have enjoyed several glasses and don't bother to undress for bed. An hour or two later I am on my knees, retching into the toilet.

"I must be seasick," I gasp when Holly comes in and asks what's wrong.

"But Lisa," she answers, "the boat isn't moving, we are still at the dock." (When I got home I told Mummy about feeling dizzy because I drank too much champagne. I decided to leave out the part about the trip to the head. "Oh sweetie," she answered me, didn't I ever tell you that if you get dizzy in bed all you have to do is stick your leg out, put your foot on the floor, and the room should stop spinning immediately.")

It is a week later, and having left Monte Carlo, Nice, and Saint Tropez behind, the *Miranda* docks in Majorca, Spain. The Colonel and another guest tell us that they have arranged a surprise for us all during cocktails on the aft deck. While we are all sitting together and eating a local fish appetizer, three handsome musicians and two beautiful flamenco dancers arrive on the boat. The men are dressed in black pants and shirts and have black hats held firmly by strings under their chins. They look like matadors, without the capes. The women are wearing bright red ruffled dresses, scarlet roses in their hair, and black shoes with very high heels. They are holding castanets in their hands. The musicians start to play their guitars and tambourines, and with their castanets clicking, the women begin to twirl their bodies, swirl their dresses, and stomp their high heels on the deck. Soon, the captain and the crew join us to watch, and one of the dancers pulls Colonel Fitzroy up out of his seat to try his own version of flamenco. After a moment Holly and I are doubled over laughing. His feet try to keep in time with the music while his arms wave in the air, and his large bald head shakes from side to side. He is trying to look suave, even a bit aloof like the Spaniards, but his face is too red and his expression too comical to pull it off. Soon the dancers, the musicians, and everyone on the deck are clapping and guffawing at his performance. After the show is over, the performers give out cards and tell us they will be dancing later that evening at a small club in town. Of course we decide to go.

The next day the captain walks into the dining room while we are having breakfast. He looks very upset.

"Last night one of my crewmen jumped ship," he tells us.

"Oh no, I hope it wasn't Hans," I chime in, thinking of the cute twenty-year-old from the Netherlands I have exchanged a few looks with.

"Well, actually yes, it is Hans," replies the captain. "He went to the club last night and became intoxicated with wine and with the blond dancer. He decided to stay here in Majorca with her. Stupid boy."

I thought about this for a minute and realized that sailors aren't the only ones to jump ship. My father had done that too, and also for a blond.

Our glamorous cruise came to an end in Gibraltar, where we climbed to the top of the famous Rock. From there we looked out across the ocean and saw the coastline of Africa. I loved the idea of being able to see another continent. The Rock is home to families of Barbary Apes, and they jumped and played around us, begging for food. One of the monkeys climbed up on the Colonel's shoulder, then perched himself on top of his shiny bald head. The ape looked as if he was posing for a picture, and I grabbed my camera, taking a final photograph of my extraordinary trip.

When I arrived back home in Maine, my friends were curious about my European cruise. They seemed bored and eager for new adventure, and I realized how lucky I had been to have had such an incredible experience. My attitude was not entirely one of gratitude, however. Two weeks on a 175-foot yacht, being waited on hand and foot, had turned me from a privileged adolescent to one who *expected* not only privilege but perfection. Several nights after I returned, Mummy, Lee, and I were having a delicious roast lamb dinner together and the cook Mummy had employed for the summer forgot the mint jelly.

"Mint jelly is *always* served with lamb," I growled. "How could Margaret forget it? How stupid of her," I added with a flourish, making my point.

Mummy slammed her fork down and said in her loudest, angriest voice, which compared to Daddy's, was not very frightening, "Lisa Barstow, I've had enough of your spoiled attitude. Ever since you've gotten home from Europe, you have been impossible. Now go to your room and think about it." At sixteen I was still being sent to my room, only this time I knew I deserved it.

Two summers later, I went to Europe again. Instead of a first-class airline ticket, I sailed on the *Queen Mary*, third-class accommodations, with several friends and a young married couple who were our chaperones. Peter was going to spend the summer tutoring two American boys at their parents' home on the Mediterranean Sea, and my friends and I had planned a few days in the south of France so that I could see him.

Before he left, we spent a romantic night together saying goodbye. I had surrendered my virginity several months earlier when several of Peter's friends were killed in a late-night head-on collision on their way back to college. After this tragedy, I realized that to deny ourselves and wait for the wedding night seemed ludicrous when a life can end in a matter of seconds. However, as mature as we believed ourselves to be, at eighteen and twenty, we were extremely naïve. It didn't occur to either of us that if we didn't take precautions there might be consequences.

After a week crossing the Atlantic, our first stop was Paris, and afterwards we went to Italy. By the time we arrived in Florence, I was beginning to feel sick, and a few days later when we got to Venice, I was throwing up in the mornings and had constant diarrhea. I couldn't eat. All I wanted was water and Coca Cola. I knew I had to see a doctor, and the hotel found one for me. He prescribed antibiotics and told me in his broken English that I was too sick to be traveling. I was very frightened and wanted to go home, but I was too weak to fly such a long distance. It was decided that I leave the group and take a flight to France and stay with Peter. He would put me on a plane to the U.S. when I was strong enough to travel.

Peter met the plane in Nice and drove me to Saint Jean Cap Ferrat, where he was living. I felt so relieved to be with him again and knew he would take care of me. "The family is away right now," he told me, "but I called to ask about you staying and they are delighted to help. They have recommended I call their doctor, and he is coming this afternoon."

I was so weak when we arrived at the villa that I had to go right to bed. My room was in the guest house that was next to the pool, and while I lay there in the large bed, I stared at the ceiling. There were murals of flowers and nymphs bathing by a lake, and animals dancing in green grasses, with brilliant colored butterflies scattered all around. The scene reminded me of some of the allegorical paintings I had studied in my art appreciation classes. As I looked around the room, I noticed that the headboard and all the furniture in the room had been painted with flowers as well. I ran my hand over the sheets and felt the crisp, cool linen and the scalloped edges embroidered with multi-colored flowers. My head was surrounded by six soft pillows, and my body felt as though it was melting into the goose-down duvet. We didn't have duvets in America, and the fluffy down filling felt new and very luxurious. I faded in and out of sleep until the French doctor arrived. Peter brought him into my room and watched by the door while the doctor took my pulse and felt my forehead. Then he asked Peter something in French.

"He wants to know how you feel," Peter translated.

"Terrible," I groaned. "I have absolutely no energy, no appetite, and I am bleeding from my rectum."

The doctor put a thermometer in my mouth, and after a few moments he took it out and looked at it. "*Mon Dieu!*" he exclaimed, looking very upset. He said a few more words to Peter, and now Peter looked upset.

"What's wrong?" I asked, feeling alarmed.

"Lisa, your temperature is 105 degrees."

I slept for several days, waking only to take the antibiotic powders mixed in Perrier water or to go lie on the chaise in the pool house where monkeys swinging on vines were painted on the walls. This was the most romantic place I had ever been, and the doctor had diagnosed my illness as amoebic dysentery, which wasn't very romantic. I had never been this sick, and as much as I wanted to get better, I had no choice but to rest and get my energy back. By the end of the first week on medication, I was feeling stronger, and I asked Peter if we could take a drive to see the gorgeous scenery on the Mediterranean coastline. "We'll drive up the coast on the Moyenne Corniche to Monte Carlo, then come back. If you're feeling up to it, we can stop for lunch at a little café down by the harbor in Cap Ferrat," Peter told me as we got into the car.

The Moyenne Corniche is one of the three roads that wind around the mountains in the south of France. There is one at a higher elevation and one below, and they all have spectacular views of the Mediterranean Sea and the Riviera landscape, splashing their charm and bright colors around every corner. While we drove, I regaled Peter with stories of my last trip to Monte Carlo, and although we were not in a convertible, I couldn't help but imagine myself as Grace Kelly driving on the narrow hairpin curves with Cary Grant in the movie *To Catch a Thief*.

As we pull off the road and park the car next to a small restaurant, I realize I am feeling hungry for the first time in two weeks. I haven't been able to keep anything in my stomach except soup or dried toast, and I decide it's time to be adventurous. I'm so happy to be outside the villa's walls to see other people, new sights and sounds. The picturesque café is situated on the harbor, and there are brightly painted fishing boats tied up to the wharves. Blue and white checked tablecloths cover the small round tables, and colorful umbrellas are stuck in the middle of them advertising Remy Martin.

"Oh that cognac," Peter laughs, noticing the umbrellas. "The French say it is a *digestif*. Maybe you should try some?" he adds with a wink. When the waiter comes over I order a salad *niçoise*, and instead of cognac, which I detest, I decide to join Peter and ask for a glass of Pouilly-Fuisse.

"Do you think that's a good idea, Lisa?" Peter says, looking concerned. "I was only kidding about the cognac, you know."

"I am so tired of feeling sick. Maybe it will make me feel better."

I found out quickly that wine and dysentery don't go well together and spent the next day back in bed. I knew then that it was time to get home, so I asked Peter to make a plane reservation as soon as possible. Though I wanted to get well and frolic on the French Riviera, I realized that it was going to take longer than I had been willing to admit.

A few days later, I flew into Boston and Mummy met my plane. "Oh sweetie," she exclaimed with genuine concern when she saw me, "you are so terribly thin." I immediately felt better. We drove straight to Maine, and by the time we arrived, I was bleeding so badly I had soaked through my clothes.

"Must be my period," I told Mummy when she noticed the big red spot on the seat of the car. "My system is off. I hope now that I'm home my body will get back to normal."

I was comforted being home in Maine again with Mummy and my summer friends. Unlike the last time I arrived home from Europe and found fault with everything, this time I felt only gratitude.

I got stronger each day but continued to bleed every ten days or so. *Must be my period,* I kept thinking. By October, I had stopped bleeding. No "period" since September. Only then did I begin to wonder if I could be pregnant.

MARRIAGE AND
MOTHERHOOD

IN 1964, FINDING OUT THAT you were pregnant before there was a wedding ring on your finger wasn't much cause for celebration. Certainly the image of the barefoot and pregnant bride wasn't yet a known entity; even the more liberal-minded movie stars weren't putting babies before being a bride. There were plenty of unplanned pregnancies, however, and mine was one of them. I might have been in love, but at nineteen years old I wasn't the least bit ready to be a mother.

When I told my mother that I might be pregnant, she immediately called Dr. Damon, the ob/gyn who had delivered me. I went to see him the next day, and he confirmed that the urine test had killed the rabbit. I had stopped bleeding, or so I thought, just six weeks earlier, so I was not prepared for Dr. Damon's announcement that his internal exam showed that I was a lot further along.

"Either you have a tumor or you are at least four months pregnant." I was stunned and speechless. All I could do was to stare at this handsome older man. I noticed that his skin was slightly tan and the lines etched in his cheeks and around his mouth were in all the right places. They created a cragginess in his face that gave him the look of an aging movie star instead of just an elderly man. His hair was salt and pepper grey and white, mostly white, and he wore wire-rim glasses on the end of his patrician nose. His eyes showed concern but were not especially kind. They were a sharp blue, and his eyebrows were thick and bushy and salt and pepper like his hair. Underneath his white doctor's coat he was wearing a navy blue suit, and the French cuffs on his shirt had gold cuff links in them. *Dr. Damon is a gentleman*, I thought. Then I remembered the story my mother loved to tell about my delivery:

"Oh, I had such a crush on that charming doctor. When I went into labor, he was at a black tie dinner dance at the Plaza, and he rushed up to the hospital to deliver you. He never had time to change out of his tuxedo." I have always found it amusing that the first person I saw when I came into the world was a handsome man dressed for an evening out.

When I got home and told my mother the news, I wondered if her first words might be, "There goes the beautiful white wedding," or "What will I tell my friends?" Instead, she walked over to where I stood by the door to her bedroom and took me in her arms, murmuring, "Oh darling, you are so young." She felt fragile in my arms, and I hated giving her something else to be upset about. We both cried for a while, and then Mummy sat up straight, setting her backbone into the position worthy of a true stoic, and began to make plans. There was no time to lose: a wedding had to be pulled off as soon as possible. I understand all about that kind of pushing through the moment to avoid emotions. It is easier to get busy rather than to allow the feelings to weigh you down. But taking quick and decisive action was also realistic and practical. The baby that was growing inside me had been kind enough not to be obvious, but that would not last much longer.

Ten days later, in an ice-blue silk suit (white would have been too virginal and at four months pregnant it was clear I was no longer a virgin) I was walking down the aisle of the hospital chapel toward my new life with Peter. My fifteen-year-old brother Lee escorted me, and my father, who was to give me away, sat in his wheelchair, with an oxygen tank strapped to the back, next to Peter.

When I called Peter to tell him I was *very* pregnant, and that he would have to postpone taking his graduate business boards because he would probably be getting married that same weekend, he was stoic and kind, like Mom. "I love you, Lisa. We'll be fine. Everything will be all right. I'll come down right away." When he arrived in New York from Hartford a few hours later, he looked grim, but resolute. I was in my mode of taking care of everyone else's feelings so I didn't have to feel my own, and because I was focusing on others, I really don't remember what was going on inside my own mind. I just knew that I loved this man, and that it helped a lot that my grandmother was his stepfather's godmother. It made it so much easier that the families all knew each other. We were "cut from the same mold," after all.

I do remember worrying about telling Daddy. His cancer had spread to his lungs, and he was in the hospital needing oxygen to breathe and a morphine drip for pain. As Peter and I sat quietly in the taxi on our way to the hospital, I thought about the fact that both my parents knew Peter and I were sleeping together, and yet I can honestly say that I do not believe either one of them warned me that without protection, pregnancy can happen.

"You look great, Daddy," I say when Peter and I walk into his hospital room. He knew we were coming, so he was shaven clean by John, his orderly. His hair is combed and his color is better, not the deathly cancer grey that I was so afraid of.

"Thanks sweetie, the oxygen has helped." I notice the clip that has a direct line to the oxygen tank attached to his nose, and the IV needle that's sunk deep into his vein. He sees me staring at it and adds, "The morphine helps too. I've finally gotten some sleep." Then he turns to Peter. "Glad to see you my friend, to what do I owe this visit?"

"How are you feeling, Mr. Barstow?" Peter's voice sounds nervous. When I touch his hand, it is ice cold. His pale face is perspiring, and his usually kempt hair is damp and sticky looking.

"Daddy," I break in, "Peter and I have something to tell you." I hold Peter's hand tightly and take a big breath. "We're going to be married." We stand there in silence for a long moment. I can hear the whoosh of oxygen on its way to my father's lungs and a taxi cab honking intermittently outside on Amsterdam Avenue. Finally Daddy speaks.

"Well, I know you two are in love, so why not plan a wedding? Do you think a June wedding?" He attempts a smile, "I should be much better by then."

"Mr. Barstow," Peter replies, as we take a few steps closer to the bed, "we're planning a wedding a week from now. We'd like it to be here in the hospital chapel so you can give Lisa away."

Daddy looks at Peter, then to me. "What on earth do you mean?"

"Dad, I'm pregnant. You're going to be a grandfather in March." I am feeling sick to my stomach, and I sit down in the chair next to the bed. I am concentrating on Daddy's eye patch that looks like a big black dot in the midst of all that hospital white. I can't look at him in his good eye, and I am screaming inside my head for someone to say something. Finally, with a great deal of effort, my father swings his legs over the side of the bed, taking care to straighten his silk paisley robe. He stands up, and Peter moves closer to help balance him. Daddy puts a hand on his shoulder.

"Peter, I've known you and your family a long time. As Lisa's father, I should give you a punch in the face for getting my daughter pregnant, but all I want to do is shake your hand." Then he extends his right arm out to the father of his future grandchild, and to the man who would take his place in my life.

My parents rose so graciously to the occasion, and so did Peter and I. But, as I walked down the aisle at nineteen years old to become the wife of a college senior and a mother in five short months, there was no denying the fact that I had, unconsciously and unwittingly, made a choice. I had no sense whatsoever that when I left my mother's home pregnant, I was paradoxically choosing a life of familiarity and stability that would define me for many years.

Here are a few things I remember best about the reception after the wedding:

The beautiful wood paneling in the hospital boardroom where we ate cake and drank champagne.

My mother, in her pink wool dress and matching pillbox hat, standing beside my father in his wheelchair. He is wearing light blue Brook's Brothers pajamas and a silk robe, with an ascot covering his gaunt neck. Both of them look so genuinely happy.

Daddy toasting Peter and me and saying that he bet he was the only father of the bride to give his daughter away in pajamas.

My grandmother Gommy, and Peter's step-grandmother Granny, best friends for years, sitting on the couch together, laughing and looking very pleased with the turn of events.

Peter's mother, whom I had known since I was four, dressed in pink like my mother, doing her best to look happy. She didn't know how to deal with my pregnancy and hadn't told Peter's two younger brothers yet, so they weren't there.

I remember my maid of honor, my best friend Glenny, wearing a dress I had loaned her (pink again), doing what she has always done best: being a friend who loves me unconditionally.

My aunts and uncles were there, and my stepmother, Fritzi, took all the photographs. This was one event she didn't miss.

And of course, my handsome husband, dressed in a dark blue suit and wearing his blue and silver striped "wedding and funeral" tie. He is looking fiendishly at me as he stuffs a huge piece of wedding cake into my mouth.

Finally, I remember our wedding night at the Plaza Hotel, where someone had tipped off reservations that we had just been married, and they moved us to an enormous suite overlooking the fountain and Fifth Avenue. When I woke up the next morning and tried to zip up my pants, I discovered that sometime in the night our baby, who had kept herself under cover until now, had grown enough so that I had to wear the maternity dress my mother had had the foresight to buy and pack in my suitcase.

I remember being relieved to have a wedding ring on my finger, happy that I was starting a life with Peter, worried about Daddy, and sad for Mummy because she wouldn't have me for a roommate any longer. Mostly, though, I remember worrying that I wouldn't be a good enough wife or mother. But just like my mother, I knew how to be stoic, and I convinced myself that as long as I acted grown up, everything would be fine.

In March of 1965, Peter and I became parents to our first child, a beautiful daughter we named Sabrina, after the movie with Audrey Hepburn. During most of my pregnancy, we lived in a furnished rental apartment near his college campus and right across the street from the hospital where I would give birth. The apartment had been tacked on the back of a house that faced the street, so it jutted into the parking lot where cars came in and out, and the neighbors' underwear fluttered on clotheslines in the yards next door. The floors throughout the rooms were brown speckled linoleum that curled at the edges, and the furniture was old 1950's style that had yet to become "retro."

Every few days or so, I would call my mother in New York and ask her how to cook a ham or make a white sauce, and finally she sent me a Fanny Farmer cookbook with a note that told me to use it as a "bible for cooking." Peter was going to classes, writing his senior English thesis on James Joyce's *Ulysses*, and I was spending the last few months of my pregnancy learning about keeping a house, making batches of brownies (for which I didn't need the cookbook) and eating them. Peter and I enrolled in an American Red Cross class on infant care and bought a life-size doll to practice on. The fake rubber baby helped give us confidence and made Sabrina's imminent birth seem more real.

We were at my father's home in Connecticut when I went into labor. Daddy was in remission and had been spending time in the country with Fritzi. He looked stronger and more relaxed, and we were all relieved to be able to put his cancer in the background for a while and focus on this new life that was about to emerge. Peter and I drove the 45 minutes back to Hartford, and just three hours later, Sabrina was born. She arrived on the Spring Equinox, the first day of spring, and I have always thought of her as a fresh new breath of spring.

Peter waited in the "father's lounge," chain smoking Marlboro's while I was in the labor room, drugged with Demerol. I was knocked out with sodium pentathol and completely unconscious when the nurse wheeled me into the labor room. Mummy had made it clear that "if you don't have to feel any pain, then don't." I had no reason to disagree, and neither did the doctor. Given the drugs, Sabrina spent the first two days of her life in an incubator.

A few days after we arrived home from the hospital, Daddy and Fritzi came to visit us. They brought Iranian caviar, the large grey kind, which is the best, and champagne to toast our daughter and my father's first grandchild. She would be the only one he would ever hold in his arms. He died at home four months later when the three of us were visiting him once again. Fritzi came upstairs to tell me he had passed away. It was just before dawn. After I sat with my father's body for a while, I went back to bed and lay there on my back, crying softly so that I wouldn't wake Sabrina, who was sleeping next to me in her carriage. Peter had already gone back to sleep. New light began to creep through the window, and the silence of the night gave way to bird song; just a few at first, then a burst of joyful sounds filled the air. In that moment I knew that my father's suffering was over, and I was so grateful that he was free. He had lifted out of a diseased body, and I could feel his soul perched in the tree just outside my bedroom window.

After Peter graduated from college, the class of 1965, we moved back to New York with our new baby. He began business school at Columbia, and I began life in Manhattan as a young matron. Two years later, after Peter found a job as a management consultant, we bought a large apartment on Park Avenue. Then we happily decided to have another child. Our second daughter, Elise, was born in April 1968. She was a precious baby, and I was so happy that Sabrina had a sister. Beforehand, Mummy kept telling me that I needed someone to help me, and I listened to her, once again. So we hired a German baby nurse who totally took over for three terrible weeks. The nurse told me the reason my daughter cried a lot was that she was hungry. I had better stop breast feeding and let her give the baby formula instead. I listened to her also. When she left, I finally began to feel like I was free to be a mother to Elise. But I didn't put mothering first, really. Peter and I loved our girls very much, but we had been thrust into a Manhattan lifestyle that we both knew well and had no reason to believe that there might be other ways to be. We simply lived the life our parents had, the life we had grown up in.

During the Christmas season, the year I was twenty-three, I cooked a suckling pig. I massaged its little back with oil, stuck cranberries in the holes where its eyes had been, and opened its mouth just wide enough to insert a bright red apple. Before I brought the animal to the dinner table, I decorated the silver platter with holly and put the cranberry necklace I had made around its neck. The ten guests we had invited *oohed* and *aahed*, and said all the right things like "How on earth did you manage this?" and "What a dramatic presentation. Aren't you amazing, Lisa." I was very pleased with myself. We had a dining room that was large enough for my grandmother Gommy's antique dining table and twelve chairs, the set of Royal Crown Derby porcelain that I had inherited from Nanny was displayed on the sideboard, and four Steuben crystal candlesticks we had received as a wedding present flickered brightly from the center of the table.

Everyone was dressed in silk or velvet, including Peter, who wore his father's burgundy velvet smoking jacket and needlepoint slippers with martini glasses on the toes. I wore a silver *lamé* hostess gown that my mother and I had picked out at Bergdorf's, and I had expertly teased my hair, adding a "fall" so that it would look thicker. I felt a bit uncomfortable trying to manage a well-oiled and greasy pig in this outfit and was horrified when, just before the critter was fully decorated in its Christmas finery, it slipped out of my hands and crashed to the ground, its new cranberry eyes popping out onto the blue tile floor. In those days I didn't know about taking a deep breath, so I took a big sip of scotch instead and picked the pig up, trying not to saturate the silver *lamé* with grease. It was at this point I realized that the animal I had just roasted felt like the same weight as Elise. With the pig back on the platter, I walked over to the wrapping from the butcher to see how many pounds it was. Sixteen—exactly what little Elise had weighed the last time we had gone to the pediatrician. I was glad I hadn't thought of this when I was putting the pig into the oven.

This was a time of enormous upheaval in the world and in our country. Peter's stepbrother was shot down and killed flying a Marine helicopter in Vietnam. We were completely shocked. I suppose the war hadn't seemed real until this happened, and we traveled to Washington for his funeral at the Arlington Cemetery. Bobby Kennedy and Martin Luther King were assassinated not long after Elise was born, and after Kent State and

the Democratic Convention in Chicago, it became more difficult "to go back to sleep."

Peter and I went to see *Hair* and *Oh Calcutta* and the Rock
Opera, *Tommy*, by The Who. We began putting our Herb Alp-
ert records away and listened to the Beatles instead. I started
volunteering at Head Start on the lower East Side, having decided to forgo a membership in the Junior League, and I helped
out at Sabrina's nursery school, the same one I had gone to less
than twenty years earlier. Then we saw a wonderful movie,
called *My Dinner with Andre*. At the end of their dinner together,
Wally Shawn turns to Andre Gregory and says, "Why is it that
so many people I know talk constantly about leaving New York
and starting a better life somewhere else, but no one ever gets
up and leaves? It's like they are living in a self-imposed ghetto.
They want to leave, but they can't."

Soon after that, Peter and I began to imagine a life outside
of the city, and in 1970, we left Manhattan and moved to a
home in the woods north of Boston. I had lived in New York
for twenty-five years. It was time to begin a new chapter.

GRIEF

TOMORROW IS NOVEMBER 20, 2007, and it will have been twenty-five years since Peter passed away, a silver anniversary of time gone by. Our son, Adrian, was just nine months when the cancer entered our lives. He is twenty-six now. Our daughters are grown women, and our oldest grandchild just turned sixteen. I have been married to Bill for fifteen years, and in three years I will have been sharing my life with him longer than I did with Peter. After all this time, what is my need to write about his cancer and death all about?

It is about telling the truth. Peter's death blew me apart, and the pain I felt has been a great teacher. Since his death, I have spent many moments reliving the nine months of illness leading up to it, the agony of letting him go, and how our family coped with the loss. I began a journal the day I waited at home for the pathology report, and in it I recorded my fears and my rage at cancer. I also wrote about my great hope that God would not let us down. I was thirty-seven and he was thirty-nine. We had a young family. Of course we would have a future together. It was too unbearable to imagine otherwise. I prayed to God to heal him. I bargained with God, believing that, after losing my parents to cancer, I wouldn't lose my husband also. I told God that my father was one year old when his father died, and that my son wasn't going lose his Daddy at the same age. The story wasn't going to repeat itself. I believed, once again, that I was in control.

At this moment, I am feeling some resistance to revisiting that painful time and knowing that this incredibly intimate part of my life will soon be in a book, and out in the world. But, as I look more deeply, I can see that what I am afraid of is my own vulnerability. Exposing my feelings, especially in public, was not something I was encouraged to do growing up. Thankfully, I am no longer bound to my upbringing. I have been creating my own life story, not anyone else's, and my story would not be complete without writing about 1982.

We had moved to Boston from Beverly six years earlier, and were supposed to go to a dinner party around the corner from our house on Louisburg Square on Beacon Hill, the same day we heard the awful news. From the moment we heard the diagnosis, that a malignant tumor had broken through the colon wall and spread to the liver, I took over. "Well, of course we won't go," I murmured through my tears. "I'll call Natasha and tell her what is happening."

"Oh dear, I'm not sure I'm ready to tell the neighborhood," Peter said, looking forlorn and scared.

"We have to tell people, Peter. This isn't something you keep secret." Peter half-heartedly agreed. Never mind that we might have spent a few days alone with this devastating news. The girls had just been told, and they needed more time to assimilate this before their father's illness was public knowledge. I feared assimilation. It would mean I would have to allow the terror I was feeling a place to live inside my body. I couldn't sit still in my own skin and be with my despair. Peter was dealing with similar emotions. As soon as he was able, he carried on with business as usual. Rarely did we go into our hearts and cry together. We had no idea how to prepare for something as enormous as a prognosis that gives you a year, if you are lucky, to live.

"The tumor looked like someone went in and poured gasoline on it," Peter's surgeon told us after they had removed part of his colon. "It was like a wildfire. We removed as much as we could. The only way we can treat the liver is with chemotherapy." The oncologist we were referred to had devised a pump that administered the medicine 24 hours a day through a needle in the clavicle vein. I was taught to change the dressing and insert a new needle each day.

Our beautiful baby boy, Adrian, turned a year old the day Peter came home after his surgery, and his sister Sabrina was seventeen the next day. Elise and I had made a big sign that said "Happy Birthday" and "Welcome Home," and Peter didn't mind when we put a band with glittery letters saying "Celebrate" on his head. Just a year earlier we had all been celebrating Adrian's birth and Sabrina's sweet sixteenth in the maternity ward at Brigham and Women's Hospital. This year our celebration was bittersweet. The surgery was over, the pump with the chemotherapy was in place, and we were all together. We knew that we had a lot ahead of us, but we were hopeful that by the next year the cancer would be in remission and we could move forward without its presence in our lives.

Sadly, this was not to be.

Peter died eight months later, six days after our eighteenth wedding anniversary. On our anniversary, our daughters brought two red roses and placed them in our silver bud vase. They put the vase on the bureau in our bedroom, where their father had been since the last trip to the hospital a few weeks earlier. The roses were beautiful, with soft, crimson velvet petals and tall, strong stems. "Happy anniversary," they said softly. We all knew that this anniversary would be our last, and we couldn't talk about it. Oh, to have been able to talk about it. I should have been braver, one of us more courageous. Our girls were waiting to meet us in the truth, but we never met them there. We all desperately needed to hold each other, to grieve, to bond as we said goodbye. The next day the flowers did what we could not. Overnight one of them died, the blossom drooping on its stem. The other rose stood straight, having reached its full bloom. I always thought that the one that died was a prophecy of what was to come. Now I wonder if the one that lived was really Peter's.

The memorial service was held at Trinity Church, a historic Episcopal church on Copley Square in Boston. It was the church where we worshipped as a family. Sabrina and Elise were confirmed there, and Adrian had been baptized in the chapel less than nine months earlier. In the days after Peter died, I found much solace and support from our minister, and I was gifted by many moments of grace, feeling a soft tranquility between the jagged edges of grief. I inhaled these moments like someone drowning and gasping for a few more seconds of air. Grace Air. It held me long enough to create a service that I knew my husband would be happy with. I wanted his thirty-nine years to be celebrated with joy, and God led me to grace that showed me the way.

Trinity Church is large, and it was filled. The school Elise attended, and where Peter served as treasurer of the Board, canceled its ninth grade classes and bussed our daughter's friends into the city for the service. Instead of wearing black, I wore a bright red wool print dress that Peter had bought me at a boutique on Newbury Street. It was very expensive and French; I knew he would be pleased with my choice. After the service, people came back to our house and I stood in the front hall hugging everyone who walked through. Tears kept streaming down my cheeks as I told everyone how lucky I was to have had him as my husband. I didn't realize that a reception line had formed until someone came up to me and said, "Lisa, look outside." I noticed that it was raining hard when I poked my head out the door. A long line of friends stood together on Louisburg Square, and the line went all the way down the block to Mt. Vernon Street. They were waiting, under umbrellas, to come into the house. No one seemed to mind.

Three days later, Lee and I are driving with the children to Maine. Peter's ashes are in a box on my lap. We have called a friend who has a lobster boat to ask if he will take us out so we can scatter the ashes into the bay in front of our house. This was Peter's wish.

When we get to the dock, our tiny son, Adrian, stuffed into a snowsuit and life vest, is handed down into the boat. My brother's long arms reach out to grab him, and he places him safely next to his sisters on the bench. I am holding tightly to the box. It is freezing cold, and the water on the bay is as grey as the sky. Our friend, Goldie, who hauls traps all year round, is used to being out on the water at this time of year. We only know a summer bay, filled with sunlight and warm wind, and water a pale, shimmering blue that matches the sky. The old lobster boat chokes and sputters for a moment and then the engine catches and we glide out the gut into the bay. Storm clouds are gathering above, and once we are past the shelter of the land we are met by a frigid wind.

"Smells like snow," Goldie yells above the noise of the engine. Soon we are far enough out so that the boat is in line with the shore and our summer home, the Casino.

"Here, stop here," I call out. Goldie steers the bow into the wind and cuts the engine. I have brought a prayer book and ask Lee to read the passage for the "burial at sea." Sabrina and Elise are holding onto their baby brother and each other. A strand of blond hair has broken loose from under Elise's wool cap, and she absently brushes it out of her face, wet with tears. As my brother reads the service, I walk to the stern and open the box. Inside is a plastic pouch full of grey ash. I tip it toward the water and slowly spill the ashes into the current that flows out to the sea. My body is shaking, and I am wondering how I can let it all go when I look up and see a seagull flying toward us. Once he is over the boat, he turns sharply and flies in the direction of the current where the ashes are drifting. I let them all go then. At that precise moment, the beacon on the lighthouse nearby begins to flash and soft snowflakes start floating, like feathers, out of the late afternoon sky.

"Oh look, everyone," I exclaim through my tears," the first snow." The Spirit of the natural world has given us a gift—more grace.

"Sure is, the first snow of the season," Goldie answers, and I notice that tears are sliding down his cheeks as well. He clears his throat and glances back up at the sky. "Ready? Better get that little guy in before it gets much worse."

"Ready?" I turn to the girls and hug them and my son to my heart.

"Oh Mom," the girls cry, "Daddy really is gone."

Back in Boston that evening, Lee and I are sitting in front of the fire in the living room. The girls and Adrian are sleeping upstairs. I open the box for the last time and pull out the pouch. I stare at it, but I can't bring myself to put my hand inside and touch the small bit of ash and tiny fragments of bone that are lying at the bottom. Nothing makes sense. I don't want it to. If it did then I would have to admit that this ash is all I have left of Peter's body. I can't do that, not now. I stand up and go over to the fireplace. "Dust to dust, ashes to ashes," keeps repeating itself in my mind. Then I take a deep breath and throw the plastic pouch and the box into the flames.

Nine months later

Paying the bills, feeding the baby, another load of laundry—please God, help me to breathe awhile longer—but then night comes and I slide into grief again. There's Peter on the family room photo wall, alive, grinning at me. Then in an instant the wall caves in and tells me the truth. He's dead. He is never coming back. This world I am in is alive, and it is alive without him.

He is never coming back—the wail distends my belly, my breath is stuck in my heart. I am not sure I want to be in this world without Peter in it. How can it possibly be? I press my face into the pillow on the couch that propped up his exhausted body those last few weeks. I can smell the cancer. I turn away and pace the room. Like a big cat who is beginning to understand she is trapped in a cage. A prison of grief separates me from the world.

I have been laboring so hard to climb out of this despair. I will need to birth myself out of the valley of the shadow, someday I will need to.

I absolutely do not know how to do this. Is this a test of my animal instinct? Am I to smell and feel my way through this loss? To follow a scent, or a touch, that will help me survive? My eighteen-month-old son helps me. He is a strong light in the midst of all this darkness.

Adrian looks up at me and says, "Dada in my heart." A few weeks ago, when he asked, again, "Where Dada?" I told him that his Daddy was in his heart, and now he says it nearly every day. His tiny fingers always point to his heart that is being filled up with his father.

I'm in the bedroom, sorting through Peter's clothes. . . . Adrian wanders in—and moments later there is a tiny blond boy swimming in a sea of silk ties. "Dada's ties"—he looks up at me, so pleased with himself. He has tipped the mahogany tie rack over and is lying on his stomach, arms and legs outstretched, moving like a fish through water. He feels the silk close to his skin. "Dada's ties," he tells me again. I sit down with him and put the ties around his neck one at a time, like leis, until they come all the way up to his chin. He giggles, "more."

"No more, sweetheart." I hold him tight, heart on heart, trying to ignore the pain I feel in my heart knowing my son won't remember his Daddy.

Peter is here with us, of course, but I am so fucking angry that I cannot touch him, hear his laugh, or watch his blue eyes squint narrow when the laugh turns to uncontrollable giggles. I can't push my fingers through his graying curls either, or sit and have a great conversation over a delicious meal and a bottle of really good Bordeaux.

I am like that cat. I have figured it out and I am wild with rage. OK, OK, don't go too far. . . . There's a place beyond that I dare not go. I am a Beacon Hill matron, a former Sutton Place resident and debutante, for God's sake. We are not supposed to get too raw.

April 1995—thirteen years later

I have returned home after spending three weeks in New Mexico at a writing retreat with Natalie Goldberg. I gave this trip to myself to celebrate my fiftieth birthday in June. While I was in the Southwest, I became entranced by the landscape's powerful red rock energy and felt myself opening to its mysteries. I attribute the following communication to the Spirit of the land. It guided me to write this letter to Peter, and to hear his reply.

Dear Peter,

Lately, in my journey, I have been working with the fears I have about death. What is it like to be dead? Dead—that word will not stop stalking me, death will not leave me alone these days. I am obsessed with it. I understand with my mind that the separation we feel between life and death is really an illusion, but I want to believe it in my heart. Peter, what I want to know is where you went, where do any of us go when we leave the Earth, this place on which our physical bodies have been living? What happened to you that November morning in 1982? What were you trying to tell me when you kept pointing to the picture window in the bedroom? I thought you were saying "slide," so Lee and I removed the pillows from behind your head and gently slid you down so that your body was flat on the bed. This is my belief. Is it real or a delusion? Like the breath in yoga, your spirit wanted to travel unimpeded through your body one last time. A final breath, sinking into bone—surrender—so peaceful—as your spirit left your body, moving toward the sky on the other side of the window. Once born out of the body it is free to be everywhere.

But you tell me, Peter, what is death? I am ready to listen. I have moved my anger aside, thanks to a lot of hard work. You seem surprised. Anger? How could I be angry when it was you who got sick and died? You left us. I wanted to grow old with you, to raise our son together, to watch our daughters become women, be grandparents together. You have a piece of me, my youth. I hadn't

*ventured out on my own before we married. I was a child-woman, unlived, not
yet seen. I was more yours then than I would be now, if you were still my
husband.*

I want to ask you one more time, Peter, what is it like to die?

Dearest Lisa,

*So, you want to know about death? It is intangible, an experience of being free.
Not free like flying, free like no mind. It is possible to collect yourself on the
head of a pin and at the same time be as vast as the Grand Canyon.*

It doesn't hurt.

*There have been times when I have been near and you wouldn't let me in
because you had too much fear. There is no fear here. How can you feel fear
when you have died and survived?*

*Death is another womb, Lisa. But this time your birth pushes you out into
unlimited love and limitless space, without the density of earth and without the
ego running the show.*

*Your work with shamanism has been helping you to understand the im-
portance of dying consciously. It is necessary to keep your own "container" as
you pass into the void. Your consciousness is part of all creation. We are all
part of God.*

*When we die, the body breaks open, becomes brittle, and deflates without
breath. It turns static, dry. Blood, fluids, muscles, bones, organs, dry up without breath. Like an apple sucked dry by frost; or a pod that was home to the
milkweed before it escaped on the wind, heading for home. Home, Lisa, that's
what dying is, it's Home.*

*Of course you wonder why I had to leave our home so soon to go to an-
other. Why did I leave you and the children when there was so much living left
to do? I cannot give you a good answer to that. Ask yourself why some apples
stay on the tree all winter long, why babies begin to crawl, or why people love
to laugh. Instead of asking "why," try asking "how" did I leave you instead.*

OK, Peter, how did you leave us?

I left you with sorrow, Lisa. I left you grieving. I had accepted my choice, though. The place I had come to, the work of my soul in this lifetime, was completed. I left you physically, but I haven't left you and the children.

Peter, I hardly remember you. Sometimes our life together seems like a dream, another lifetime. I want to know you now. I want to reach in and touch the core of you that I know has blossomed like a pond lily in summer. I want to hear your voice.

You do, Lisa, when you are still.

Yes! It's true. I can hear you and see you. I still love you. I naïvely thought that when I gave my heart to Bill I would stop loving you. But how could that be? I didn't understand then there is no limit to the love we can hold in our hearts. Love has no beginning or end.

Just like what we call death, Lisa. There is no separation, no beginning or end.

2006—nine years later

I had a vision during a therapy session in late October. Peter appeared to me as if in a dream:

He is sitting at a café table, wearing his favorite orange sweater. He looks up when I walk over, and in that moment I know that it is time for me to let go of him again. I have been walking the cycle of life and am on another place on the spiral. I am going deeper into an awakened self.

"I have been living a new life," I tell him. "I want you to go on your own adventures. You can leave if you want to. You do not need to be here with me any longer. Thank you for being here, dear Peter. This is your time now." He looks at me as if to say "Are you sure?" I nod. Then he stands up and a sailboat appears. He steps on board and goes right to the helm, peering out to sea. He turns to me and smiles broadly, looking excited about his voyage. "I have loved you all my life," he says as the sails catch the wind and the boat sails away. I am sobbing as though he had just died. Only this time I am crying tears of gratitude that he had stayed so long. This is his time for his spirit to be completely free of the past.

I am in a trance when I leave the therapist's office. I know what I have to do, and drive directly to the Casino. It is a glorious fall day, and I sit down in one of the blue Adirondack chairs on the knoll overlooking the bay. A moment later, I turn to look at the harbor and watch as a man in the distance hoists the sail on his sloop and casts off the mooring. I can see that he is dressed in something orange. An orange sweater, perhaps? The sailboat comes about and heads out toward the passage that takes you to the sea. Then, as if out of nowhere, a lobster boat appears, and the two boats pass each other directly in line with where I am sitting. It is as if Peter's ashes that I tossed off the stern that day in 1982 had materialized into this sailboat with a man at the helm. I leap up out my chair, waving, screaming, "*Bon voyage dear Peter, bon chance . . .*" and I watch, stunned by the power of the Mystery and the Spirit made manifest, as the boat disappears behind the island and sails out to sea.

Several weeks later—November 20*th*
The twenty-fourth anniversary of his passing

I decide to drive to the beach for a walk. There is a chill in the air, but the sun is dancing brilliantly on the dark blue sea. As I walk down the beach, my eyes scan the horizon, and I see a boat. A lone sailboat way off shore, its sails filled with a strong wind, moves quickly through the water. I look at my watch. It is 10:35 AM, the precise moment when Peter took his final breath. This is my moment to exhale and set us both free. Once again, Spirit is showing me that there is no time or space. The separation we perceive as real is only illusion. Thank you, God.

FINAL BREATH

IT IS JULY 1983, AND I am alone on a beach in Oregon, walking in the raw strength of its southern coast. I am screaming as loud as my voice will allow, aware that my screams are drowned out by the deafening clatter of chopper blades not 20 yards from where I stand. The helicopter hovers, a man points to something in the water, motions to the pilot to go lower, then jumps out and into the ocean. I begin to scream when he lifts the dead body of a young man out of his resting place, where he was nestled between two rocks near the place where the sea meets the sand. The drowned man looks like the paintings of Jesus after he was taken down off the cross, his long, dark hair streaming behind him and his chalk-white body limp, lifeless. Not an hour has gone by since he disappeared while swimming with a friend. Except for the cold of the ocean, his body is probably still warm.

I notice that the wind from the turning blades creates a whirlpool where the body has been, and I wonder how it would feel to be sucked down inside the circles, with no way to get free. Then I understand that I have been pulled down into a whirlpool of grief, and instead of a Coast Guard helicopter, only God and the passage of time would bring me up and out of the eddy of despair. This drowning reminds me of my own.

It has been nine months since Peter died, and I have taken our daughters and one of their friends on a two-week drive up the Pacific coast from San Francisco to Vancouver. Adrian, who has recently turned two, is being cared for in Maine while we are gone. Sabrina is eighteen and not happy about being along on this trip. I must have worked hard on her, probably used some guilt to get her to come: "With Daddy gone, we've got to stay close—connected as a family—especially for Adrian's sake. He's got to grow up with a feeling of family."

Sabrina's anger was the right instinct. I needed to be in control, to feel some stability, and appearing to be a family in tact gave that to me. I had no idea what I was setting up. Nothing wrong, I suppose, but not what an eighteen-year-old wants to feel responsible for. Elise is fifteen. She is feeling the pain of her father's death deeply. Both girls are grieving, confused, and angry. They have been sweet in their caring of me, Adrian, and each other, but this trip has taken them out of familiar territory. It is tipping us all off balance. What are we doing enclosed in a car, driving hour after hour looking at scenery that has a wild, harsh beauty, when what we need is a journey that is gentle and soft? I suppose that part of the plan was to test myself. Was I going to be up to arranging and completing a trip like this on my own? I was thirty-eight years old, and ever since I was married, every trip I had taken had been with Peter.

I watch as the helicopter hovers, suspended in one place, while the body is brought up in the metal basket to the open door. Once he is inside, the helicopter banks sharply to the left, away from where I am standing, and flies north, following the coastline. Rooted to the beach, I watch it disappear. Then, as I turn to walk back down the beach, I see Elise jogging toward me.

"Oh Mom, where have you been? We've been so worried." I fall sobbing into her arms, and she holds me. I am stripped of my ability to be the stoic and protect her from what I have witnessed. I tell her the story. More pain. I think about the drowned man's mother getting the call. I feel surrounded by death and wonder what it is that God is trying to tell me. My fifteen-year-old daughter has her own questions about death, but I lean on her now.

I have turned to all three of my children in the twenty-five years since their father's death, and there have been times when I was too dependent on them. In some respects, we have grown up together. As an adult child of alcoholics, I spent many years trying to become an adult and leave the "child" behind. I believed that things *should* be a certain way for my children and for me and have had some difficulty separating my life from theirs. I called it love, when at times it was control. One year for my birthday Peter gave me the poem about children by Kahlil Gibran. I had been trying to give Sabrina more space to grow as a young teenager, and it wasn't easy for me. She wasn't happy being told who she should be. Gibran's poem says that your children have souls and paths of their own, that "they are not your children. . . ." But I held on. I couldn't imagine her as being separate from me.

When Sabrina went through a divorce a few years ago, I wanted to clean up the messiness for her. I tried to be her advisor, her best friend, her comforter. I wanted to be in the loop, so I called a lot. I worried when she was feeling down and I worried when she seemed "too" happy. A therapist I know told me that I was trying to fill the hole in the role and be her "perfect husband." I was also trying to make up for the soothing I didn't do enough of when she was a child. Whatever I tried came from a loving and caring heart, but I did spend a great deal of time focusing on her life, instead of my own. I thought it was my job, and I blamed myself, in part, for her suffering.

My three children's presence in my life has been a true gift of joy. But, until recently, I have been afraid to let them go. Not because I believed they couldn't make it without me, but because I have been afraid I couldn't make it without them. Now, I know that it is time to take one final breath and transcend my attachment as the "keeper" of my adult children. I'll begin by inhaling the fresh breath of an unattached and unconditional love. Then love will be transformed.

AVALON

I MADE THE DECISION TO leave Manhattan with Adrian after watching street cleaners mop and brush a stream of blood into a storm drain on West 86th Street. We were on the bus going to his kindergarten, and had we been a half hour earlier would have witnessed the shooting. This gruesome scene was one of several I had encountered in the mid-eighties that convinced me New York City was not the place I wanted my son to grow up. It didn't matter that we were living in one of the West Side's most beautiful buildings with Central Park directly across the street. I didn't feel safe.

A series of synchronistic events, and listening closely to my intuition, led me to Amherst, Massachusetts, a small college town west of Boston in what is called the Pioneer Valley. I felt like a pioneer. Adventurous, courageous, and independent. I had a destination, but the life I was going to was unknown territory. I would have to create it for Adrian and myself. I had completed a training in body-mind therapy and was waking up and exploring many alternative ways of thinking and being. I needed a new community that would support these changes. When I told friends I was moving again, after just three years in New York, they accused me of being a nomad. But as I look back on June 1987, I can see so clearly that my soul directed me from the home of my birth to a home of new beginnings. If that is what nomads do, then so be it. I was wise to take the risk and follow my heart into a new physical landscape and into a new landscape for my soul as well.

The girls were in college and had summer jobs lined up, so it was just Adrian and I who climbed into my new bright red Subaru station wagon, which the doorman and I had packed so full, my big stuffed teddy bear's face was pressed flat against the back window. Then we said our goodbyes and headed out of the city on the West Side Highway.

June 2008—twenty-one years later—in Amherst at Peg's

Dearest Peg, my dear friend and neighbor, my first friend in Amherst. You were the kind of neighbor I had always dreamed of having. Thank you for being there when I knew no one. How many cups of coffee have we had at your kitchen table trying to sort ourselves out? Ten years older, full of experiences I had never had, you helped open me to a life of new beginnings. Thank you.

I remember when we sat on the deck of my small house next door to yours and plotted to blow up the huge new Victorian that was being built in front of us, blocking our beautiful view of the Pelham hills.

I had fallen in love with the land before us and tried to buy the twelve acres of fields and orchards the previous year while I was looking for a home in Amherst. I was surprised when the property went to someone else. I felt so connected to the land and had been sure I was going to live on it. When the realtor showed me the house next to yours, I bought it because it backed up to the orchard I loved. I envisioned building a contemporary house with large windows facing the hills, certainly not a Queen Ann Victorian.

"Imagine anyone building a Victorian in the middle of an apple orchard," you said with disdain.

"Peg," I answered, "what I hate is that every day this house just gets bigger and taller. I agree, let's blow it up."

A few days after this conversation was the first time I saw Bill. He was perched on a beam that ran across the length of the Victorian's second floor, eating his lunch. I walked down to get a better look at the house and heard a friendly "hi!" coming from above. I looked up, and there was this very cute guy grinning down at me.

"Oh hi," I scowled." How much bigger is this house going to get?"

"My name is Bill," he called down, ignoring my question and my expression. "I'm the foreman on the job. Would you like a tour?" He helped me as we climbed around on the framing. There were no walls, so every room had a perfect view. Bill told me he loved this place so much that he came early every day and sat for a while, enjoying the scenery before he began his work. I had to admit that he was building a beautiful house.

In October of that year, the man who had hired Bill to build the house decided not to move in and put it on the market. The next day he had three full-price offers, and one of them was mine. Peg was away, and when she returned I told her to come right over, I had some news. We wouldn't have to torch the house after all. I'd be moving in instead.

When my offer on the house was accepted, Bill was the one I worked with to complete the interior of my new home. He reminded me that if I wanted wiring for stereo throughout the house it would be best to have him do it before the sheet rock went up. We were in the master bedroom, and I said I'd like to have speakers in there. He asked if I wanted them in the bathroom also. No, I told him, the bedroom would be enough.

"Oh," he said, "I think you'd like them in the master bath as well. When you are shaving it would be nice to hear the music up close."

"But I don't shave, and I don't have anyone in my life right now who does," I replied.

"Nevertheless, I think you will be happy that you put them in." He wired the bathroom and installed small speakers. Two years later it was Bill who was shaving and enjoying the music.

After getting to know him while we worked on the house, I decided I'd like to get to know him better. I asked him to a dance recital and while we were having dinner, found out that he had gone to the same prep school as my daughter Elise.

"What year did you graduate from Holderness?" I asked him.

"In 1975," he replied. Now I have never been very good at math, but I figured out pretty quickly that if I had graduated from high school in 1963, I was twelve years older than him. *Oh this will never work*, I thought. But I had already begun to dream, no, I mean obsess, about us being together. It was like the land. I was sure he and I were meant to have a future with one another. I was smitten by his smile, his kind eyes, his humor, his good looks, but more than that, I felt that my heart had guided me to him. He didn't know this, and I didn't tell him then. He wasn't ready, and I realized after a few dates that neither was I. I had let go of my attachment to the land, and it came back to me with a house on it. Then, I let go of this man, and two years later he came back to me with an open, ready heart.

I named the property Avalon, after reading the book, *Mists of Avalon*. Avalon was the island in King Arthur's time that was home to the priestesses who worshipped the Goddess before the patriarchal church moved into England. When I looked Avalon up in a dictionary, it said "a place in an apple orchard, facing east." Bill had made a sunburst out of shingles that he placed over the front door that faced the East; and the orchard the house was nestled in had been planted the year I was born. I am convinced that the land is sacred, and I believe its spirit created the magic that brought Bill and me together. It also helped make Avalon the special place that it was.

I wanted to share my home and build community, and the Apple Blossom Festival was Avalon's debut. Peg, and her Holcomb clan, helped me create a gathering one weekend in May when the apple trees were in full bloom. My friend, Kiera Skiff, an opera singer I knew from New York, arrived Friday with her accompanist for an evening of arias. The concert was preceded by a dinner that we cooked for twenty-five guests. The music was beautiful, and a perfect way to begin the festival celebration.

The next day there were belly dancers, jugglers, mimes, and pony rides out on the lawn in front of the house. A friend brought her bagpipes and played at the top of the driveway, which had the desired Pied Piper effect, and soon a large group had gathered. One of the loveliest sights of the day was the arrival of a beautiful young woman dressed in a white gown, riding through the fields bareback. She had long, dark hair, and her horse's coat was shiny and well brushed. When she arrived at the edge of the lawn, she slid off her horse, leaving him to graze under the laurel tree, while she walked through the crowd. I don't know who she was, and neither did anyone else. But her appearance at the festival could have been a scene from the Avalon of long ago.

I began hosting workshops and trainings in the Animal Totem Process, with Steve Gallegos and in Ericksonian Hypnosis, led by Mel Bucholtz. I sponsored one in Rubenfeld Synergy Method at UMass for my teacher Ilana Rubenfeld and hosted a reunion of Return to the Earth, our Colorado vision quest group. I held a Native American pipe ceremony, and a fire walk that the chief of the Amherst fire department asked his firemen to attend, hoping it would help them with their fear of fire. I was seeing therapy clients in the little barn I had remodeled, and Peg facilitated sessions there in Spiritual Emergence. This work, devised by psychiatrist Stan Grof, brings a person to an altered state by breathing deeply and rapidly while listening to evocative music. This practice can help free the ego by providing images from the unconscious mind. My friend Sally set up her teepee on the land behind the house, and we held drumming circles there every week.

During all this community building, Adrian was growing up. One weekend when I needed his bed for a guest, he told me that he didn't want strangers sleeping in his bed anymore, and that he wasn't too happy living in what he called "a center." "I just want our house to be a normal home," he said. After that things slowed down at Avalon. Bill moved in with us in 1991, and Adrian, his twelve-year-old friends, and Bill's two sons, Joe and Dan, took over the attic for video games and ping pong. All the wonderful workshops and gatherings had run their course over the four years since I had bought the property, and Avalon began a new chapter.

Dearest Bill—as I sit here at Peg's, there are pink and white peonies in a vase on the table next to where I am writing. They remind me of our wedding. On each table there were round glass vases that held large bunches of peonies. Your mother and sister Cathy helped arrange them. You are off in Kauai, and I am

here remembering the scent of all our Junes in Amherst: peonies, mountain
laurel, wild roses, French lilac; blossoms that opened to the solstice and our
wedding day, nearly sixteen years ago.

In 1992 Bill and I were married beside the water garden we had
created. It had a small waterfall that flowed into two small
ponds, and the water was re-circulated by an underground
pump. The frogs didn't know it was man-made. They found
our water feature the moment it was filled and enjoyed resting
on the lily pads that we had planted. We stocked it with tiny
fish, and birds dropped seeds into the ponds so that soon there
were tall cattails growing out of the water. Iris, beach rose, and
miniature azaleas bordered the edges of the water garden, and
one of the apple trees created shade from the summer sun.
Adrian's piano teacher, a versatile musician, brought her harp,
and her husband played his classical guitar while Bill and I
walked behind our five children to the flagstone terrace where
the minister stood. Our white Samoyed dog Tate was right
there in the middle of it all. He stood next to the minister,
looking like the best man. We had invited fifty of our dearest
friends and family, and they listened to us say our personally
written vows to one another.

Bill and I lived at Avalon together for seven years, then the
nomadic life called once again and we left for Maine. Adrian
had graduated, like his sister and stepfather, from Holderness
and was on his way to college, as were Bill's sons, and Bill and I
were ready for a change. Maine was my childhood summer
home, and I had always felt a yearning to live there year round;
and we both wanted to live near the ocean.

The final event we had at our home in the apple orchard
was a "high tea" and dharma talk by our friend, Tibetan monk

Tulku Thondup. Tulku had been introduced to us by our dear friends Eileen and Dechen Latshang. Dechen and Tulku lived together in a monastery in Eastern Tibet as boys, and in 1957, when it was no longer safe to be there, they and many other monks fled the Chinese, taking months to walk over the mountains into India. This gathering was really hosted by Eileen and Dechen, and the money that was raised was donated for the rebuilding of the monastery after it had been nearly destroyed by the Chinese.

All our furniture had been moved to Maine, so except for the rented tables and chairs, Tibetan banners, prayer flags, and the beautiful tea sets that Eileen had collected for serving tea, the house was empty, devoid of material things. It was winter and the apple trees were bare, but a few frozen apples, shriveled and dried, still clung to the branches, and I thought, *What a perfect metaphor for grasping.* This place was not an easy place to surrender. I was letting go of a home I had found because I had been courageous and listened to my heart. Avalon's spirit had supported me and helped me become more of who I wanted to be. It was a place that opened its doors to so many interesting and gifted people, a home where my family and friends could come for renewal, and the house had been built by Bill. Avalon brought me to Bill.

Now, with the Buddhist belief in impermanence floating through the empty rooms, I had no choice but to let go, and as I did, Avalon disappeared into the mists. The couple who purchased the property uprooted the mountain laurel by the front door, covered the water garden with dirt, and completely remodeled the house. The pale blue Queen Ann tower room was gone. The wrap-around porch where we had sat so many evenings watching the moon rise and the fireflies dance, gone; and the deck off the master bedroom where Bill and I sipped coffee, watching as the red-tailed hawks soar over the field, gone as well. The blackberry bushes that our dear dog Tate used to feed on, gingerly removing the berries so that his nose wouldn't be stuck by the thorns, have grown completely wild so that the opening from Avalon to Peg's property is blocked. But the beautiful larch that stood beside the house is still there, and the apple tree that shaded the water garden is firmly rooted; and as I write this, I can see a hawk circling above the land.

Nothing ever remains the same, and Avalon will live in my heart forever.

BILL

MY HUSBAND IS A PATIENT man. Yesterday he lay on his back for several hours painting the underside of a pipe to protect it from the heat of the Hawaiian sun. He had to squeeze his six-foot body between the pipe and the ground that was covered with sharp gravel, and after some time, he realized that the small stones were digging themselves into his skull. So he painted with his right hand and used his left to cradle his head and hold it up in the air. I think that this is the same pipe he had wanted to get inside, seated on a skate board, and ride through it for hundreds of feet from beginning to end. "To make sure there are no obstructions," he told our brother-in-law, who is his boss. Fortunately, the request was denied. Later, Bill confessed to me that he had imagined the ride through as a kind of shamanic rebirth. He had a caesarian birth fifty years ago and thought that the pipe might serve as a new birth canal.

My husband is a romantic man. Whenever we hear our favorite songs "When You Wish upon a Star" or "Over the Rainbow" or best of all, Louie Armstrong singing "What a Wonderful World," he scoops me up in his arms and we dance. I watch big tears slide down his cheeks, and I wonder how I was lucky enough to find this man.

He has brought me dozens of roses over the years. Sometimes after a big fight, reminding me of forgiveness and generosity. He has taken my hand and led me into gardens filled with gorgeous flowers, remarking on their beauty and teaching me their names. A few years ago, I accidently ruined the Pueblo wedding vase we had given each other when we were married by putting water in it to hold flowers. He took it over to his shop in the barn and glued all the shattered chips back on. Then he painted it with a new coat of special black paint. There was no fanfare. He quietly put it back on the shelf and waited until I noticed that it was as good as new. He does things like that a lot. Fixes things without an expectation of praise or thanks.

Bill loves music, plants, cooking, Tai Chi, science fiction, and kids. He is the Pied Piper grandpa for the children in our family. Our youngest grandchildren call him Boo. When he plays with them he gives them his undivided attention. Nothing else gets in the way, and they trust that kind of presence, focused and complete until it is time to come to an end. I have seen him play a game of monopoly all afternoon into the evening, and continuing the next day. Did I mention that my husband is a competitive man?

He is passionate about music. For seventeen years I have been living with my own personal deejay. He seems to know what music goes best with whatever activity we are engaged in, always setting the right mood. He usually prefers jazz for cooking, Miles Davis, Diana Krall, or B.B. King playing his favorite "guitar girl" Lucille. I gave him expensive ear phones for his fiftieth birthday, and I love to watch him as he plugs himself in, kicks off his shoes, settles himself onto the couch, sliding his long legs out straight, and closes his eyes. The look on his face is happy, content, relaxed. Then, he disappears into his music world.

Bill has loved music since he was very young. He told me he has been listening to the blues since he was ten, and he knows a lot about it. In Amherst, and throughout the Pioneer Valley he was Blue Bill and ran a popular blues program on the radio. I had never met a deejay before, and every Monday afternoon after we had begun to date, I made sure to be near a radio so that I could listen to his show. Looking back, I think I first fell in love with his deejay voice. It was not packaged or "pat" like so many radio men, but authentic and natural. He was totally himself on the air: adorable and funny, telling ridiculous jokes and lots of interesting facts about each artist. When his muse, Stevie Ray Vaughan, died, he devoted an entire show to his music and life. He told stories on the air about meeting him when he ran the UMass radio station. "That was before Stevie got sober." It was not lost on him that this tragedy was all the more poignant because Stevie had finally found freedom from his addictions. "Better to die without that karma," he admitted, after he thought about it awhile. Bill also memorialized Jerry Garcia when he passed away. He took me to my first and only Grateful Dead concert. I bought a tie-dyed tee shirt with pinks, yellows, and oranges spiraling between my breasts. We took some pot but didn't need to smoke it because we quickly got high on second-hand smoke. I am not a huge Dead fan because I don't really understand their music. I am always trying to find a melody that I can latch onto. It is a cultural thing. I was brought up on Gershwin.

When I returned to Hawaii after a month in Massachusetts my husband had bought an orchid that was in bloom. Its lavender flowers brightened up the stone wall where all the other orchids, whose blooms had ended a few months earlier, sat in pots. "I thought you would like to see at least one with color," he told me when I remarked how beautiful it was.

When we lived in Maine, we began a crystal collection and hung the pendants in our bedroom window. When the sun caught the crystals, tiny rainbows bounced all over the room and sent our granddaughter Leila into fits of giggles while she chased them, holding her tiny hands out to catch their light. Now these crystals hang on a slender thread on our *lanai*. There are twenty-four of them with one glass ruby-throated hummingbird suspended in their midst. I love watching the sun bounce off them and dance across the porch. I remember *Peter Pan*, my favorite play as a child, when Tinker Bell is dying and Peter asks everyone who believes in fairies to clap and save "Tink." I clapped and clapped because I have always believed in fairies; a good thing too, because they are alive and well and living on my *lanai*.

Bill does not compromise himself. He is his own man, and he can be incredibly stubborn. He is honest, and sometimes painfully literal. I am most comfortable in the abstract world, which makes communicating a challenge at times. We are both independent, and I am just beginning to appreciate that about us.

He hates it when I cling or grasp, and so do I. Although he is twelve years younger that I am, I find his wisdom on certain subjects to be dependable and true. I am finally getting off my high "I'm older, therefore more evolved" horse, and settling into new-found humility. I watch him. So content, sometimes annoyingly good humored, and I have thought *denial*. Maybe he isn't really in touch with himself. Now, I wait a moment before I make that judgment and try to imagine how lovely it would be to be so unencumbered.

He is getting better about listening to *my* wisdom, as long as I don't try to force-feed it to him. We have been learning about ourselves through one another for years, and sometimes I wish I didn't have so much to learn. I almost wrote "we," and I heard my husband whispering into my ear: "You take care of Lisa and I'll take care of Bill." My ability to project is legend.

Bill has a kindness that reaches deep into his cells. He is without guile. His thirty-three year practice of Transcendental Meditation keeps him in the moment, and, in turn, has helped me to understand that the moment is all we have. During our years together, my heart has opened, not only to him, but also to myself. I can allow myself to be vulnerable and am not as afraid to trust. Now, when we fight, I don't need to be so defensive, or judge him like I did before. So he can trust me more, as well.

Is he a knight in shining armor? Thank goodness, he has shown me that there is no such thing. Bill may not be my rescuer, but he has helped prevent me from going back to sleep.

RELATIVES

I AM SURE IT COMES as no surprise that the political animal in my family was an elephant, and that most people I grew up with thought that donkeys were asses. I doubt that my grandparents or parents knew any Democrats, and if they did, they weren't discussed. Because everyone was of the same political persuasion, I don't remember any passionate arguments. Arguments of any kind were frowned upon anyway, unless they were behind closed doors. There was one passionate political family story, however, that has left an impression on me:

My grandmother Gommy's sister, my Great Auntie Too, was married to a man who announced one night at dinner, "If Roosevelt gets in for a fourth term I'm going to shoot myself."

A week later, after the Democratic victory, he went up to his bathroom, put a gun to his head, and pulled the trigger.

When I heard this, I was truly horrified that someone would actually take his life because of a Democrat. But what impressed me the most was the lack of outrage or shock expressed on the part of my family when they related this terrible incident. It seemed to me as if they weren't entirely sure he hadn't made the right decision.

I remember the women in my family shaking their heads and clicking their tongues about Eleanor Roosevelt. They gossiped that she was much too aggressive for a woman and was "so terribly unattractive." I wonder now if they hated the Roosevelts because they believed they were traitors to their class.

I liked Ike. When I was seven, my friends and I sang a jingle to the melody of the popular song "Whistle While You Work." It went like this: "Whistle while you work, Stevenson is a jerk, Eisenhower's full of power, whistle while you work." During the 1952 Presidential campaign, I wore the Republican Party campaign button to school every day, and I remember after the election hanging outside my fourth-floor bedroom window waving a small American flag at Eisenhower's cavalcade as it sped down Sutton Place on its way to the United Nations. His limousine was open air, so I could see him easily. He was standing up in the car, waving and smiling to all the waving, smiling Republicans in my neighborhood, and he looked so fatherly, so protective, that I wrote an emotional story about our president and shared it at school.

When JFK was elected, some of my family's distaste for Democrats mellowed. Here was a Democrat, after all, who was married to "one of us." Jackie had gone to boarding school with younger sisters of my mother's friends, and my grandmother, Gommy, had known Jackie's mother in Southampton when they both summered there.

"Thank God that dreary Mamie Eisenhower won't be first lady anymore," I remember my aunt saying. "Jackie is so beautiful, so cultured. She'll set things straight."

I wanted to question their ideas, but I learned at an early age that it wasn't safe to disagree with the opinions of family members, especially during the cocktail hour. Mummy told me once that when she was in boarding school she had a history teacher who spoke with scorn about capitalism and how a socialist society cared more about the equality of its people. His lectures had her so convinced that when she went home for Christmas vacation she brought up the subject at family dinner.

"Your Papa listened quietly," she recalled, "and when I was finished telling everyone that I thought capitalism was unfair, he put his fork down on his plate and told me that if I really thought that, then he would be canceling my allowance, since it was because of capitalism that I had one." Then she added, "I took his comment seriously. He knew that I wasn't about to go without my allowance, and I knew that things were done one way in the family and that being impressed by socialist teachers was not the way."

Lolita

I had an aunt named Lolita who was as exotic as her name. My mother's brother, Uncle Jimmy, met her while he was married to Sophie, who was French-Egyptian and eight years older than he was. I remember Aunt Lolita telling me some years later that the moment she met my uncle, she knew he would be her husband one day. I was intrigued by Lolita from the moment I met her. I had been ten when Sophie and Jim were married and was so in love with Aunt Sophie's accent that I sobbed when my mother informed me that I would never ever have an accent like that. Oh—her voice was so dramatic, romantic, and foreign. I was mesmerized. But when my uncle left her for Lolita, I abandoned Sophie and her unattainable accent, and true to the fickleness of youth, my loyalties shifted to this younger, more glamorous woman who soon became my new aunt. Everyone in the family seemed relieved.

Although she was from a traditional East Coast WASP family, she had spent much of her twenties in Europe, one of three dazzlingly beautiful sisters who, I imagined, had left broken European male hearts behind. She wore peasant skirts and espadrilles, huge tortoiseshell sunglasses like the French women vacationing on the Riviera in Mom's *Town and Country* magazines, and she looked extremely trim in Italian pants and sweaters, before Italy had moved into Madison Avenue. But I especially loved the large gold hoop earrings that dangled from her ears. Not one woman in our family had pierced ears. I was quite taken by the possibilities that presented themselves to me because of my new aunt's untraditional and international style. Was it truly possible to be exotic even though my mother's image presented itself as the 1950's staid, conservative matron? I may not have been born with a sexy accent like Sophie, but I certainly could look the part. My Aunt Lolita showed me that there were possibilities for a more dramatic future appearance.

When Aunt Lo was pregnant with her second child, my cousin Lela, she was mistaken for Jackie Kennedy, who was pregnant with John John. The two women shared the same wide jaw line, almond eyes, and bouffant hair style, and when my aunt donned the then stylish pillbox hat, you would think that they were identical twins. It was plausible that the First Lady might be visiting Manhattan, and when my uncle took his Jackie look-a-like out for an elegant dinner, the celebrity-seeking clientele were abuzz.

My parents spent a lot of time with my aunt and uncle when they still lived in New York. I remember standing around in the kitchen with the four of them while my mother fixed dinner, everyone telling stories, mostly hilarious "bad boy" stories about my uncle. I had always thought of Uncle Jimmy as a rather mysterious man. He was elegant and suave but not too approachable, at least to a young child. Compared to my mother's other brother, my Uncle Jack, who wrapped me up in big, generous hugs, Uncle Jimmy seemed more remote. For much of my childhood he was a bachelor, living in California (he roomed with Hoagy Carmichael for a while) and didn't have his own children until he was in his forties.

"Jimmy, you were a hellion on wheels," Mummy announced to us all in the kitchen that night. Then turning to me: "One night, when he was eighteen or nineteen, after nightclubbing around the city, he stole a taxi cab. The driver had gone into a corner store to buy some cigarettes and had left the motor running." I stared at her.

"Why did you do that, Uncle Jimmy?" I was shocked.

"Because you had too much to drink, right, Jim?" Daddy replied.

Then, not waiting for his answer, Mummy quickly changed the subject. Looking over at her brother with amused affection, she said, "Tell Lisa about the time you took the pig to the dance."

"Well, you know," Uncle Jimmy began, laughing to himself, "your grandmother and my Daddy, your real grandfather, had a farm outside of Philadelphia that we all went to on the weekends." I nodded. I had heard stories about the beautiful farm on the Brandywine River where my grandfather kept race horses. "There were horses, mostly, but the farm had other animals like geese, chickens, and pigs. Your Nanny told me I had to go to a dance at a community club down the road, and I didn't want to. I was very angry at her, so I decided to try something guaranteed to get me kicked out."

"What was that?"

"I went to the pig pen and took one of the piglets, then walked to the dance with it under my arm. When I got there, I hid in the bushes and slathered grease that I had brought all over the little pig. Then I stepped into the hall and let the animal go." Everyone in the kitchen was laughing hard now.

"What happened?" I asked, not sure whether it was time for me to laugh yet.

"Oh, that piglet made a racquet, squealing and running all over the place. The grownups tried to catch it but couldn't hold on because of all the grease. Kids were falling down, sliding around on the floor trying to grab it. . . ."

"Did you get kicked out?" I asked, eager to find out what happened.

"Oh yes, and Nanny was told that under no uncertain terms would I ever be invited back," he said, chuckling.

I began to imagine this scene at my dancing school in the ballroom of the Colony Club. I could see the girls with their organdy dresses up around their waists, the boys in their navy blue suits lunging at the pig, the very proper instructor falling in the grease, his black patent leather shoes trying unsuccessfully to get a footing on the dance floor. I joined the adults and began laughing hard also. Then I thought about my uncle and the taxi cab, and stopped laughing.

"So, what happened when you stole the cab?" I asked a moment later. Everyone stopped laughing then, and waited for my uncle to tell me the end of the story.

"When the cab driver came out and found his taxi gone, he called the police. They located the cab I was driving and chased me for a few blocks. When they caught up to me I was arrested and spent the night in jail." This was beginning to sound serious, not funny like taking a greased pig to a dance.

Mummy continued, "The next day the headline story on the second page of *Daily News* read: *Son of wealthy socialite and Presi-*

dent of American Electric Power jailed for stealing a city taxi cab. We were raised to believe that your name never appeared in the newspaper unless it was a marriage announcement or your obituary, and this was quite scandalous. Your grandparents were extremely upset."

"Did you move to California after that?" I asked, wanting to change the subject. "Tell me about the time you roomed with Hoagy Carmichael."

A few years before he and Aunt Lolita were married, Uncle Jimmy had his first heart attack, and after the second one, when he was in his early forties, he and his family moved out of Manhattan, doctor's orders, to a quieter life in Vermont. He was told to give up smoking and alcohol, which he did, for a while. Then he began collecting expensive Dunhill pipes and sweet smelling tobacco. He had us all fooled until we realized that the iced tea he was drinking was full of rum and called "Long Island Iced Tea." My uncle was the kind of man who didn't want to live his life by rules, even though they might have helped keep him alive longer. He died of a massive coronary at forty-nine, alone by a beautiful mountain lake, putting food out for the wood ducks. I was shocked that anyone could be home in the morning, eating eggs and toast with his wife and children, kiss them goodbye, with a "see you at lunch" over his shoulder, and never come back. Cancer doesn't kill that quickly. At least you have a chance to say goodbye.

Aunt Lolita and my two cousins stayed in Vermont after Uncle Jimmy died. They came to Maine in the summers, and Aunt Lo visited us in New York. After my mother died in 1972, I began to think of Lolita as a surrogate mother. I was still impressed by her glamour that seemed enhanced by the move to the country. Her velvet pants and large gold jewelry stood out in the simplicity of Vermont. Her old friend Bernard, the suave, perennially tan French-Egyptian, who had worked in Sophie's antique shop and unwittingly introduced Lolita to my uncle (Bernard had always been in love with her) became her "beau" for the next few decades until she died.

By then, I had seen past the glamour. For years my beautiful aunt had worked hard to keep up the appearance, but back pain and excruciating headaches left her helpless. She became powerless over the drugs she took, and toward the end of her life it was difficult to know whether her pain was physical or mental. My exotic, glamorous aunt had disappeared.

The picture of Aunt Lolita that I want to remember her by is the one taken of her at the helm of my uncle's sailboat, *La Golondrina*. She has a colorful bandana wrapped around her hair, and her large sunglasses are shielding her eyes from the summer sun. To her left is my uncle, smiling up at his beautiful wife. They both look so happy, and when I look at this photograph, I think of this moment as being their own personal Camelot.

Lee

I am not sure how to write about my brother Lee. Every time I think of something to say, it seems trite or somewhat condescending. I am four years his senior, and there have been times in our past where I have definitely played the older sister card. After our mother died, leaving us orphaned at twenty-seven and twenty-three, I began to play the co-dependent mother card as well. Over the years, we have both worked hard on healing our sibling relationship, separately and together; and as a result we have grown to be good friends and often seek each other's counsel. I have turned to him for comfort, wisdom, and more faith. He helps me to know myself more intimately. After all, we were conceived, and grew, in the same womb. But, as with most siblings, our roles and experiences growing up in the same family were vastly different. In our "looking good family," John Bradshaw, the author of *The Family*, would label me, as the oldest child, the "good girl hero," and Lee as the "scapegoat and rebel."

I suppose the way to write about my brother, as he begins his sixtieth year, is from the perspective of a dear friend whom I have known for that many years. It is amazing to think that our aging process has gone well beyond Mom and Dad's, and we, not our parents, are each other's model for old age.

My brother is studying to be a minister. He is a wonderful writer and speaker and has already given many sermons at his church in Amherst, MA, as well as in other churches in the area.

He works in the development office at Amherst College and knows so much about computers that it seems they are a part of his nervous system.

He is married for the second time and has fathered four beautiful children.

Lee is "waking up" to the fact that he is very, very smart. For years our father's voice kept him shackled in a deep place of shame and lack of self-esteem. When I think of my brother as a child, I see his sunburned and peeling pug nose, his white blond hair and dark brown eyes like Mom's, and his zest for life. But I also see his vulnerability in the face of our father's uncontrolled rages. Today, he is a man who has faced the demons he once screamed about in his nightmares. My brother has developed a strong spiritual connection that continues to help him transform and grow. I would say that his shoulders, once rounded and collapsed around his heart, are now straight and strong, and his great big heart is exposed and wide open.

Lee has been wise counsel to my three children when they needed a father figure to turn to. He has spent over twenty-five years in recovery and follows a twelve-step path, which in my opinion, is a good path for living whether there is addiction in a family or not. He has generously shared his story when he thought it might be helpful.

We all know that he is there for us, no matter what. Lee was by my side when Peter died. The day after the burial at sea, he came over to the house with friends from Arica, his spiritual school, and they stayed up all night praying for Peter as he journeyed through the Bardo, believed by Tibetan Buddhists to be the stages or realms of the afterlife.

Twenty-seven years ago, my brother had to endure what people say is the hardest loss a person can go through: the death of a child. Serena, his nine-month old daughter and first child, came down with a virus that exposed an untreatable heart defect. She slipped away several hours after having a spinal tap to determine her prognosis. Lee and his first wife Alice were left in stunned agony. Their daughter, who had come down with what they thought was her first cold, was with them one day and left them to go back to God the next. My son, Adrian, was born several months later, and Lee and Alice had a second child, a son, Taylor, a year later. Our boys are best friends and business partners now.

On the lighter side, my brother organized a beautiful surprise fortieth birthday party for me, and he and my sister-in-law Cynthia surprised me again twenty years later at a fabulous party for my sixtieth. Recently, he took the day off from work and invited me to go with him to the Norman Rockwell Museum in the Berkshires. We laughed and cried as we saw Rockwell's images of our 1950's childhood. Its culture was portrayed with humor and depth, and we remarked that we must be "getting on" to be so moved by an artist we once considered overly sentimental.

In my opinion, Lee is already a minister. He is a good listener and counselor and has a caring nature, especially with children and elderly people. There have been times in his life when he has been "to hell and back," so he knows about humility, which is essential to the ministering of others.

I am proud to be your sister, and I extend my admiration and love to you, dear Lee.

Will, my brother Lee's son, who is now fourteen

My nephew Willy has a grey plastic sword and a shield. They were all he wanted for his third birthday. That was four months ago. Since then I have never seen him without them. His sword and shield occupy their own place at the table at every meal and are propped up against his bed every night when he goes to sleep.

Willy is a warrior. When he holds his sword, he assumes the true warrior stance. He places his feet firmly on the earth, legs slightly bent, arms outstretched, head high, his body in readiness for a duel.

"I kill dragons," he tells me, tossing his blond head just a little.

"Oh Willy—thank goodness there is a dragon slayer on Bay Road. Now South Amherst will be safe from fire-breathing dragons." He looks hard at me to see if I am kidding. "I'm serious, Willy." Then a small smile of triumph passes over his sweet round face. "Aunt Issy, do you really believe in dragons?"

Willy is not only a warrior. I think he knows something about being a shaman, as well. I remember when our family spent a wild winter afternoon in our attic at Avalon. There were five children under the age of six who, after several days of Northeast cabin fever, were taking on the energy of the jungle. So we brought out the drums. Two homemade hoop drums, an African jimbay, a tom tom, and rattles to shake. The kids and four adults began moving to the drumbeat—hopping, jumping, rolling, dancing, laughing, and singing. . . . Screaming jungle power!

Then I noticed that Willy had left the group. He was lying on his back, alone in the corner of the room. Instead of his shield, he had placed my hoop drum on his chest and was beating the drum slowly and rhythmically. His eyes were closed. I knew he had left the room and was on his own journey. Perhaps he was in the rainforest or sitting on the Plains of the Southwest. Where are you, shaman/warrior boy? What wisdom will you share with me? Soon, I will tell you that shamans can talk to dragons.

For my granddaughter, Leila, while observing Queen Anne's Lace

Delicate sweet child of grace—Welcome! You are as lovely as a field of Queen Anne's lace: stems so straight, so green and firm, they hold the gentle blossom that is you. Their roots are buried in the earth. Your roots are from your ancestors whose past holds you in the moments of this life. I see tiny flowers that create the larger bloom, each with their own stem that holds fast to the center. Mirror images of their host, a burst of beauty, just like you!

We are in the meadow dancing in the wild flowers. Bewitched, you turn to me and curtsy, your hair bright yellow like the sun: then, laughing, you surround yourself with lace, a fairy's dress. Surely you are a bride of this landscape.

For my granddaughter Allison

Make me sweet again.
Fragrant, fresh and wild
and thankful for any small event.
—Rumi

Watching my twelve-year old granddaughter Allison leaping, twirling, dancing through the pinks and reds of sunset was no small event. We were standing on the knoll beside the bay, awe-struck by the evening's color, its vibrancy reflected on the shallow water that barely covered the flats.

"Allison, this is the most beautiful sunset I've ever seen."

"You always say that, GranLisa."

"Well, this time it's the truth." I looked over at her and could see that she was as full of wonder as I. Then, without a word, she jumped down onto the rocky beach and ran barefoot over stones and onto the mudflats. Running out to catch the colors of the evening in her arms, she became a silhouette against the magenta sky. Embraced in a wild sweetness of freedom, she leaped in the air and danced, and I saw the promise of childhood, the fresh, unselfconsciousness of youth, moving in grace and beauty at the end of the day.

PILGRIMAGE

SEVERAL YEARS AGO I MADE a pilgrimage to the island of Iona on the West coast of Scotland. It is the place where St. Columba traveled from Ireland, bringing Christianity to that part of the British Isles. Pilgrims from all over the world visit this tiny island to feel the presence of Jesus and experience the thin veil between the material and spiritual worlds.

While I was there, I met a lovely British woman, an artist in her nineties, named Violet. She had been to the island many times. I loved her description of a pilgrimage: *The place does not matter when you seek the peace and adventure of a pilgrimage. I mean it doesn't have to be beautiful or labeled as sacred. The white wall of a monastic cell or the untouched canvas will do. As an artist, any blank surface excites my mind. That the attempt is always imperfect matters not. The blessing of the pilgrimage is in the aspiration.*

My aspiration had been to deepen the heart of Christ in my life, and while I was there, His strong, clear light filled me again and again. I had felt a fear of death before I left, and soon after I arrived, I understood that it was ego death I was afraid of. I asked Jesus for a renewed commitment to Him, and everywhere I walked on the island I felt the grace of the sacred blowing light through my hair. Poised at the edge of a brilliance that took my breath away my reality moved between form and spirit. I was standing at "the place where the two worlds touch."

At twilight I sat beside the sheep in their pastures, and God told me that they were holding Christ's light for healing in the world. I felt so thankful for their offering and was deeply moved by their presence.

I found a smooth blue-grey stone on the beach and carried it with me until the day I left, when I returned it to the Bay at the Back of the Ocean. I breathed a prayer on the stone, and a piece of my heart, so wide open by now, stayed with the stone on the beach on Iona. Then I, like so many pilgrims, brought the Holy Spirit, manifest in the sacred light of Iona, back home with me.

I have been on an inner pilgrimage for most of my adult life, and unlike the outer journey, the inner one has no destination, beginning, or end. When I choose to be aware, I feel myself walking the spiral path that leads me deeper into the landscape of my soul. I co-create the inner pilgrimage with my body, mind, and spirit, and my journey to Iona helped me find a clear and perfect union of all three.

HOUSE OF CARDS

July 2006—in Maine

I have been hearing God whispering Rumi's poem "Don't Go Back to Sleep" in my ear for some time now, and this morning I awoke to the breeze at dawn and a seagull drifting past my bedroom window, calling my name.

I jump out of bed, make a pot of coffee, and when it's ready take a steaming mug out to the knoll beside the bay. It is a glorious morning. Cool, salmon sky, half-tide, boats in the harbor turned toward the rising sun.

I am in a new time of soul growth. I am ready to let go of more illusion and step through the round and open door that separates me from God. I have to listen with a pure heart, and see with eyes not clouded by fear. If I go back to sleep, I will not surrender to the will of God, and that is not what I want.

"You must ask for what you really want."

If I go back to sleep I may lose my marriage, and that is not what I want. I want to be married to Bill, but God is telling me that what I think I want is about control and unreasonable expectations. So, as I sit looking out at the bay, I ask for answers. A few hours later I find this quote by Anthony Mello:

> *Some people will never learn anything because they grasp too soon. Wisdom, after all, is not a station you arrive at, but a manner of traveling. . . . To know exactly where you are headed may be the best way to go astray. Not all who loiter are lost.*

So often I jump right in with my own answer because it is too frightening to sit with my emotions, instead of waiting and listening for God. I fear letting go and not being in control. Now this house of cards I have been trying to keep from falling down will not stand up any longer. Bill has told me that he will not live in a house that isn't strong, or where one of us always wants to be the dealer. He has had the courage to recognize that, like the house of cards, our marriage needs a new foundation. I too have felt this over the past few years, but the difference is that I have been working on changing the marriage by trying to change him, without his permission.

He has asked me to stay at the Casino for the month. He doesn't want me to contact him. He will be in touch with me. He is claiming new territory with stronger boundaries, and I am terrified. What if the wall of detachment he has built around himself keeps me out permanently? I know Bill is frightened also. In the past he enabled me. Now he has stopped. He is giving us both some time to come back to ourselves.

I just need to settle, keep the focus on myself, and pray.

I am in the raging river trying to grasp a branch and pull myself out, fearing a freefall around each bend. When I am in this kind of water, I forget that God is the river, the freefall, and the branch. I forget all that I know because I am so scared of dying.

Now, I see that an old, tired part of my marriage is dying, and we are being given another chance to individuate and love each other more completely.

A few weeks later

We are on the Cape visiting Bill's family, and I am going to take our niece, Claire, for a swim near Wood's Hole. Joe, my father-in-law, has given me directions to a good place to swim, and as I pull into a parking space, I realize that I am at Quisset Harbor, across from the tiny Yacht Club where Peter learned to sail as a boy and worked as a teenager. It is July 14th and had he lived, Peter would have been sixty-three today. I turn toward the water and a gaff-rigged Herreshoff with a young boy at the tiller sails by. I hold Claire's hand as we cross the street and tell her: "Do you see that boat? That is the kind of boat my children's Daddy sailed when he was a boy."

"Let's go swim, Auntie Lisa," Claire replies, understandably disinterested. We climb a short hill to "the Knob" and take a swim in Buzzard's Bay. It is a gorgeous, clear afternoon, and the water is warm enough to stay in for a while. When we finish our swim and come back to the beach, we spy a huge blue crab that appears to be dead. But then Claire shrieks, "Oh look, his legs are moving." So we find sticks, since neither one of us wants to pick this creature up, and gently move him back into the water. Peter's birth sign was Cancer, the Crab.

That night as I lie in bed alone, having left Bill's family's gathering early, I remember my summers with Peter, in what seems like a lifetime ago. When he first took me to Wood's Hole, I was nineteen and Bill, who was somewhere else in the world, was seven. I am wondering if my thirteen-year-old second marriage is going to survive, and God has graced me with the spirit of my first love on his birthday. Surely this is what Rumi meant when he wrote:

People are going back and forth across the doorsill, where the two worlds meet.

When I look back on this time of crisis in our marriage, I can see that it was, in part, precipitated by the possibility of moving to Kauai, where Bill would have the opportunity to fulfill the lifelong dream of living in Hawaii and work on his family's tree farm. It was as if we were being asked to choose between two different lives that didn't connect. Although I loved the idea of spending more time with my sister- and brother-in-law, Hawaii is a long way from Maine, my family, and friends. If I was going to live in Kauai, I needed to believe that my marriage was strong enough to support the change, and Bill knew that he needed a wife who supported him, yet came for herself as well.

Over the years we have worked on our relationship with a number of gifted and wise therapists, and during this pivotal time, we had a guide who verbalized what we were afraid to admit. Our differences and our dreams had brought us to an edge where, as a couple, there was no turning back. Either we held hands and jumped into the unknown, or we went in different directions, without each other. Fortunately, we realized that either way we would be facing the unknown, and neither of us wanted to do it alone. We'd spent years developing trust and deepening our faith and love in one another, and thankfully, that is what inspired us to stay together and build a new relationship.

Since 2005, Bill had been working on building us a new home in Maine. We designed the house ourselves, making sure its construction was solid. Rather than a house of cards, our home, with its strong foundation, became the new metaphor for our marriage and our future life together.

Free Write:

Leaving soon for Kauai—January 2007

The familiar patterns of my life are dissolving into the tapestry, and a weave with a new design is beginning to emerge. God is the weaver. He and I choose the colors, the design, the weft of the threads. I have been striving so hard to create the "perfect picture," but it is just an illusion.

The Creator within beckons me: "Don't go back to sleep."

I turn to look at my life's design and I see a hole. It is another rabbit hole, and I am the only one who can enter it. It is time to fill it with fresh new awareness and life. This space in my weave wants softer colors, pale milky greens, blues, and lavenders, Easter colors. I want to fill it with creativity, not control.

I want to open like a lotus flower and fly like the heron, to be as still as a pond, then dive into its center from my place on the rim of the circle. I want the petals of my body to blow softly in sweet air, my wings to be strong enough to carry me to where I am going next.

When I leave for Kauai, I will take the hearts of those I love along with me. I will scoop them up and place them in a nautilus shell that, like me, has many chambers. The shell will find a home in my new home, and when I go inside I will remember to feel gratitude for all the blessings of my ever-expanding circle.

God reminds me that the herons always come back to the marsh and that the lotus bloom pink every year. I can fold myself into an origami bird, flying west then east, somersaulting across the sky. We are on the same earth under the same sky, and a heart filled with love can live everywhere.

KAUAI-2008

BILL AND I HAVE LIVED here for almost two years. We found a lovely house to rent and furnished it with great thrift shop and garage sale items. We are beginning to feel at home, and yet I miss the people and the landscapes that are rooted so firmly in my heart.

The island is small, but with the ocean wrapping itself around the circumference, there is plenty of space to take long, deep breaths. The other day, my yoga teacher and I were talking about the expansive beauty of this island, but when you look at it on the map, it is just a tiny speck in the middle of the Pacific.

"A small speck, perhaps, but that pinpoint holds the infinite," Ellen pronounced with her typical yoga wisdom.

"Ah yes," I replied, "there are places on Kauai that God must have visited and taken notes before He created the Garden of Eden."

In the winter months, humpback whales pass by on their way to Maui to birth their calves, and again as they return to Alaska. Tourists come to enjoy greener pastures for a while. Like cattle egret, they land and take off, day after day. When I talk to my family and they tell me they are weary of snow and ice, I don't mention that the orchids on the *lanai* are blooming or that I went to the beach yesterday. I want them all to move here so my grandchildren can run around in flip flops instead of snow boots, my son and son-in-law can body surf with Bill, and my daughters and I can go to the farmer's markets in January. I'd love for them all to breathe in the air of Aloha that circles the island, like the whales. It is the spirit of tenderness, unity, and love and its magic stirs the soul. There is a peacefulness, an unhurried pace here. Something I rarely feel back home.

This island has its pockets of darkness, however. Many young people are in crisis, due to drugs, and recently, some teenagers have taken their lives. There is racial discrimination, and the county's officials are continually "passing the buck." Change happens on "island time," and because of the high cost of living, it is necessary for some people to work three jobs to make ends meet. The rip tides and strong ocean currents claim many lives every year, and on Kauai's one road that circles the island, there are fatalities that occur with too much regularity. Paradise Lost? Not at all. There has always been darkness to contrast the light.

We had been here for vacations and had had no trouble totally immersing ourselves in the romance of the place, but *living* in paradise is another thing altogether. I was convinced that paradise would cease to exist when you actually live there. I mean you don't pay bills, take out the garbage, and wash the car in paradise, do you? After living here I have discovered that since you have to do those things anyway, you might as well do them in the serene beauty of Kauai, the Garden Isle.

Chickens and roosters live in abundance on the island. The other day when I was at Costco, I saw a tourist stopping traffic so that a mother hen could cross over the road with her three chicks. Later on, I watched the chicken training her brood to find lunch under the tables in the outdoor café. We have a rooster who wakes up and crows under the bedroom window when I get up to go to the bathroom at 2 AM. Bill says the rooster thinks the bathroom light is the sun and he's just doing what he was born to do. Lately, I have been feeling my way to the loo in the dark. When I asked, I was told the reason why there are so many chickens and roosters on this side of the island is that they were blown here from Kokee State Park in 200 mph winds during Hurricane Iniki. Now that must have ruffled a few feathers. . . .

It *is* different here. The other day an inebriated horse whisperer rode a horse into the open air lobby of the hospital, maneuvered the animal into the elevator, and went up to the third floor to visit his sick grandfather. He thought that if his grandfather could visit with his horse he would feel better. Security was alerted, and when the horse and his rider got off the elevator, they were waiting for him. The nurses wheeled the ailing man into the corridor, so he was waiting also. When he saw the horse, he yelled at his grandson: "Stupid, da horse, dat one not mine." That's local pidgin for "that is not my horse, silly."

Every day garden spiders weave new webs on our lanai. They wrap their prey in cocoons, waiting to eat it later, and yesterday I saw the head of a grasshopper poking out of one of them. When the webs begin to create a Charles Addams kind of look on the porch, I run around with a broom and as gently as possible, whisk the spiders' homes and eateries off the lanai. Each time I say "sorry spider," as if that's going to matter. I've come a long way, though. When I first arrived here I was convinced that the spider hanging from her thread outside the kitchen window was my new totem animal and tried to communicate with her spider wisdom. (E.B. White would have been proud.) Bill loves to take care of critters. He began putting food out for a feral cat we had seen running around in the yard, and each time he checked the can was empty. One night he put out left-over meatloaf for the kitty. Later on he had to go downstairs to the ground level, and I heard him laughing. Instead of the cat, an enormous Buffo toad was sitting beside the can eating the meatloaf!

Some of our friends were confused when we told them we were moving to Kauai. When they asked me how long we'd be living in Hawaii, I'd answer, truthfully, that I didn't know. I still don't. Moving so far away without a long-range plan went against the standards of my traditional upbringing. The old adage "look before you leap!" was repeated as a warning whenever any change was discussed. Perhaps a fair warning for taking risks. . . . Well, Bill and I did look. We looked hard, and decided that taking a risk and leaping would be good for us. Moving to Kauai was the next best step for our life together.

He is working doing something he believes in, and I am finishing this book. For this moment we are happy here. Who ever knows what the next moment will bring?

EPILOGUE

I HAVE NEVER WRITTEN A book before, so of course I have never finished one. It is the last day of 2008, and I am winding down this story. I have flipped around the gamut of emotions: exhilaration one minute, a sense of emptiness the next. I have been writing my story on and off for eight years. It is time to move on.

My mind races. . . . Have I written down everything that is important? Have I told the truth, with enough kindness and grit? I don't want to leave anyone out, especially the children in my family. Like my amazing grandsons, Alex, 17, who loves baseball; Jonathan, 15, a marathon runner; and darling Henry, who just turned one; and my niece Emily, almost 16, who is totally beautiful and an awesome varsity softball pitcher.

I don't think I mentioned that my eating disorder is still a part of my identity. I reached a "bottom" with my weight and joined a twelve-step program for food addicts. The disease was arrested for a while. I lost many pounds, thanks to sponsors, meetings, weighed and measured food plans, and no flour or sugar foods. I was sure I was free and believed that no food would ever again taste as good as abstinence felt. When I left the program after three years I knew I'd need to be careful, and for a while I was. Then denial took over where the control left off and I have, at the last scale reading, gained most of it back. The difference this time is that I am able to live in my body without as much guilt and shame. I am learning to see that my compulsive relationship with food has been a big part of my identity since I was born, and that when I choose conscious-ness, instead of control, I just might be able to change the pat-tern once and for all.

I am trying yoga again. I have always despised yoga because it brought me into a body that did not want to be reminded that it hurt, was fat, and wouldn't stretch like other bodies. But this time I can see that it is the yoga mind that will stretch me and help set me free. Then, all else will follow.

I am learning the importance of discipline. Instead of be-ing punitive, it is a practice in self love. I hope that my father hears this, wherever he is. He was called to deliver the message but didn't know how to teach it in the correct way. Discipline is a teacher, and when you follow that teacher you become its dis-ciple. Lately, I have been fortunate to find teachers who are helping me become more intimate with my inner disciple.

OK, so I am coming around the bend, and am in the home stretch, zooming past the wagging fingers, the "*shoulds* and *shouldn'ts*" of the past, without as much as a backward glance. I see the finish line up ahead and I can hear the cheering. This has been my marathon, my own personal best. The woman from my dream, the one I asked to teach me about courage, is there and I see that she is me. I am waiting to welcome myself home.